Gleason H. Ledyard's

TOPICAL STUDY OUTLINES

Christian Literature International

P.O. BOX 777 CANBY, OREGON 97013

FOREWORD

The most important thing in this life is to be able to read and understand the Word of God. The NEW LIFE Testament was translated so that men and women, boys and girls could read the Word of God themselves and understand what He has written, which is the Greatest of all Books.

The reason it is so important to understand His Written Word is because it shows man the way to heaven. This is worth more than any amount of money can buy. But there is much to receive in this life also. Joy and peace and happiness comes to the person who reads and obeys the Word of God.

These TOPICAL STUDY OUTLINES are a guide for Bible study. They can be a valuable help to the person, young or old, who wants to learn what God's Word says. Many Bible quotations are included, and there are many other references that should be studied. These TOPICAL STUDY OUTLINES were prepared without any denominational or church bias.

It is suggested that a NEW LIFE Testament be used for study because it is accurate and easier to understand than other translations. The same 850 word controlled vocabulary is used in these TOPICAL STUDY OUTLINES as in the NEW LIFE Testament. The use of these TOPICAL STUDY OUTLINES can be the beginning of the most wonderful experience of knowing and understanding what God has written for you to know. It can be like a blind man who starts to see. After he has seen a little, he does not shut his eyes and say, "That is wonderful. I have seen it all." He wants to see all he can. A lifetime can be spent in studying the Bible and there will be new things to learn everyday.

May the NEW LIFE Testament and these TOPICAL STUDY OUTLINES be tools to open the understanding of those who really want to know what God has for them.

Gleason H. Ledyard

Guru, Gopal. 'Maharashtra Women's Policy: Co-opting Feminism', *Economic and Political Weekly* (6 August 1994), 2063–66.

Government of Maharashtra. *Policy for Women*, Department of Women and Child Development, (1994)

Kapur, Jyotsna. 'Putting Herself into the Picture', *Manushi* no. 56, (1990), 28–37

Kavita, Shobha, Shobita, Kanchan and Sharada. 'Rural Women Speak', *Seminar 342* (Feb 1988)

Kishwar, Madhu. 'Nature of Women's Mobilisation in Rural India *Economic and Political Weekly* (24–31 Dec 1988), 2754–63

Kumar, Nita ed. *Women as Subjects: South Asian Histories*, Calcutta: Stree, (1994)

Murthy, Ranjani. 'Gender and Development in India. Centre for Women's Development Studies Report', Regional Round-Table on Women's Participation in Policy and Decision-Making Process, 10-11 October 1991, Delhi : CWDS and Friedrich Ebert Foundation

———. *Experiences and Challenges*. Chenai: Initiatives for Women in Development, (1994)

Omvedt, Gail. 'Rural Women Fight for Independence', *Economic and Political Weekly* (29 April 1989), 910–13

Poitevin, Guy and Hema Rairkar, *Indian Peasant Women Speak Up, New Delhi: Orient Longman, (1993)*

Rose, Kalima. *Where Women are Leaders*. New Delhi: Vistaar, (1992)

Samuel, John. *A Comprehensive Review of Maharashtra's Policy for Women*, Pune: National Centre for Advocacy Studies, (1994)

SHETKARI SANGHATANA

Agashe, Anand. 'Fifty Thousand Acres of Land for Women from Their Husbands', *The Independent* (2 December 1990)

Balaram, Gunvanthi. 'This Land is Her Land', *The Independent* (2 Sept 1990)

Guru, Gopal. 'Shetkari Sanghatana and the Pursuit of Laxmi Mukti', *Economic and Political Weekly* (11 July 1992), 1463–65.

Omvedt, Gail. 'Shetkari Sanghatana's New Direction', *Economic and Political Weekly* (5 October 1991), 2287–90

Somayaji, Uma. 'Land for Laxmi', *Maharashtra Herald*, (9 March 1991)

MISCELLANEOUS

Sirsikar, V. M. *Politics of Modern Maharashtra*. Hyderabad : Orient Longman, (1995)

Srinivas, M. N. *The Remembered Village*. New Delhi: Oxford University Press, (1976)

NOTE ON CONTRIBUTORS

Bishakha Datta is an independent writer and filmmaker, and one of the founders of Point of View, a non-profit organization which aims to promote the points of view of women through a creative use of media.

Meenakshi Shedde is an assistant editor at the Times of India, Mumbai and has a keen interest in visual arts.

Sharmila Joshi is a freelance writer and journalist and is the recipient of a 1997 National Foundation for India media fellowship.

Sonali Sathaye is currently doing her PhD in anthropology at Syracuse University, USA.

CONTENTS

PART 1

WHAT THE WORD OF GOD TEACHES ABOUT GOD

[*Theology*]

CHAPTER PAGE

THERE IS ONE TRUE GOD

There are five things that help men know there is a God. Not any one of these truths proves in itself that there is a God. But by putting all five together, we have proof of God's being, work and power. Each proof is like one stick. It can be broken across a person's knee. But five sticks are much stronger and cannot be broken.

The Bible does not try to prove that there is a God. Men everywhere already know there is a God, One Who is head over all things. And yet, many people wonder about Who this God is and would like to know many things about Him.

1. *MAN KNOWS THERE IS A GOD BECAUSE OF WHAT HE SEES AROUND HIM.*

How did this world come into being? It could not come into being by itself. Who made it? There is no secret about it. God's Word tells Who made the world. "In the beginning God made from nothing the heavens and the earth" (Genesis 1:1). The sky above man and the earth around him prove that Someone made them. This did not just happen. When man makes something, he uses things to make other things. But God did not use anything to make the world. "Let them praise the name of the Lord! For He spoke and they came into being" (Psalm 148:5). These things around man do not tell him Who made the world. But they do tell him that Whoever made it was very great.

2. *MAN KNOWS THERE IS A GOD BECAUSE ALL THINGS WORK AS THEY WERE PLANNED.*

Think of the earth, sun, moon and stars. They do not run into each other. They go year after year in the way they were planned to go! Millions of stars were put in their places. Nights and days come and go always as they were planned. Summers and winters come and go always as they were planned. The One Who planned all this had great wisdom. In Psalm 19:1 we read, "The heavens are telling of the greatness of God and the great open spaces above show the work of His hands." God's Word also says in Romans 1:20, "Men cannot say they do not know about God. From the beginning of the world, men could see what God is like through the things He has made. This shows His power that lasts forever. It shows that He is God."

3. MAN KNOWS THERE IS A GOD BECAUSE OF THE WAY PEOPLE ARE MADE.

The One Who brought man into being had to be greater than man. Man can know and feel and act. Man has something inside him that tells him when he has done wrong. He is not only flesh, blood, and bones, man is able to know right from wrong. This makes him know there is an All-powerful God who made man and rules over him. "When I look up and think about Your heavens, the work of Your fingers, the moon and the stars, which You have set in their place, what is man, that You think of him, the son of man that You care for him? You made him a little less than the angels and gave him a crown of greatness and honor. You made him to rule over the works of Your hands. You put all things under his feet. All sheep and cattle, all the wild animals, the birds of the air, and fish of the sea, and all that pass through the sea. O Lord, our Lord, how great is Your name in all the earth" (Psalms 8:3-9)!

4. MAN KNOWS THERE IS A GOD BECAUSE OF WHAT THE PAST TELLS HIM.

Man knows the Bible is the Word of God. Early preachers said certain things would happen in the future, and they did happen. Christ came to the earth by a powerful work to do something special for men. The followers of Christ have taken the Good News around the world through the years. Men's lives have been changed as they have put their trust in Christ. Sinful men have never been able to destroy what God has made. These things could only be done through God's power and work. "The kings of the earth stand in a line ready to fight, and all the leaders are against the Lord and against His Chosen One. They say, 'Let us break their chains and throw them away from us.' He who sits in the heavens laughs. The Lord makes fun of them" (Psalm 2:2-4).

5. MAN KNOWS THERE IS A GOD BECAUSE ALL MEN KNOW THEY NEED A GOD.

Every person knows there is something wrong in his life. He may not call it sin, but he has a guilty feeling. Every person knows there must be One Who is perfect. He knows there must be Someone Who is head over all. Man needs a leader. The Word of God does not try to prove there is a God. It just tells us about God because men over all the world already know that He is. The Word of God tells us there is only one true God. "The Lord our God is one Lord" (Deuteronomy 6:4)! (Mark 12:29b) Isaiah 44:6b says, "...There is no God besides Me." God is the Head over all things. He is the one and only God.

THE NAMES OF GOD

In many parts of the world a name given to a person has a meaning. In Bible times names had special meaning. They were given to certain people for certain reasons. The names of God show what He is like. They show how He acts and works among the people He made. Men should know what they meant to the people long ago and what they can mean today. Knowing the names of God can help man know God better. His name is greater than any other name. The Old Testament was written in the Hebrew language and the three most important names for God are in that language. The names given below are the names in English.

1. *THE THREE MOST IMPORTANT NAMES OF GOD IN THE OLD TESTAMENT.*

   A. God - This name means *The Power That Rules*. In the very first verse of the Bible this word is used. "In the beginning God made from nothing the heavens and the earth" (Genesis 1:1). This power made the world and rules over it.

   B. LORD - This name is written in big letters. It is not the same as *Lord*. It means *Life* or *The One Who Always Has Been, Is Now, And Always Will Be.* It also means *To Be* and *The One Who Needs Nothing* and *The Coming One*. In Exodus 3:14 God said to Moses, "I AM WHO I AM."

   C. Lord - This is the name which shows that God is Ruler over men and that men put themselves under God's rule and trust Him. (Genesis 15:2) It means *Owner* or *Husband*. John 13:13 says, "You call Me Teacher and Lord. You are right because that is what I am." And in II Corinthians 11:2-3 the same word means *Husband. Lord* can be used for a man, but then a small 'L' is used.

2. *THESE ARE THE OTHER IMPORTANT NAMES OF GOD IN THE BIBLE.*

   A. All-powerful God - means *The Strong One* and *The God Who Is Enough* and *The One Who Gives Strength* and *The Strong One Who Sees* and *The God Who Has Power Over All.* (Genesis 16:13; 17:1-20)

   B. Most High God - means *The Highest* or *The One Who owns Heaven and Earth.* Isaiah 66:1a says, "The Lord says, 'Heaven is

My throne, and the earth is the place where I rest My feet.' " (Deuteronomy 32:8; Psalm 83:18; Acts 7:48-50)

C. God Who Lasts Forever - means that God will never die. It also means that He is the God Who is over *things* that last forever. Psalm 90:2 says, "Before the mountains were born, before You gave birth to the earth and world, forever and ever, You are God." "You made the earth in the beginning. You made the heavens with Your hands. They will be destroyed but You will always live" (Psalm 102:25-26a).

D. LORD God is first used in Genesis 2:4. This name is used two ways: (1) God as maker of man (Genesis 2:7); (2) God as leader of Israel (Genesis 24:7; Exodus 3:15; Deuteronomy 12:1). It is used as *Owner* and *Leader* and *The One Who Saves.* And then it is also used when God talked or promised things to His chosen people. Sometimes it is written *Lord God.* This means *Owner.*

E. LORD of ALL is a name of God showing His power and shining greatness in war, and also in caring for others. (I Samuel 17:45; Psalm 46:7, 11; Isaiah 47:4)

3. *OTHER NAMES OF GOD USED IN THE OLD TESTAMENT WHICH TELL ABOUT HIM AND HOW HE WORKS.*

A. The LORD Who Will Give What Is Needed - This name means *The Lord Will Take Care of Our Needs.* This name was used when Abraham was about to give his son as a gift on the altar to God. (Genesis 22:13-14)

B. The LORD Who Heals - He is the One Who heals men's bodies from sickness and disease. (Exodus 15:26)

C. The LORD Who Wins For Us - It is God Who fights against Satan for man. (Exodus 17:8-15)

D. The LORD Our Peace - It is God Who gives peace. (Judges 6:24)

E. The LORD My Shepherd - God is the One Who leads men through hard places. (See Psalm 23 which is given at the end of this chapter.)

F. The Lord - God's Life In Us - This speaks of the day when Christ will be King of the earth, but Christ's life is now in those who have put their trust in Him. (Jeremiah 23:6; I Corinthians 1:30)

G. The LORD Is Here Now - This name also looks forward to the day Christ will be king of the earth. (Ezekiel 48:35; Revelation 11:15; 17:14; 20:4; 21:3)

H. The Lord Is The One Who Sets Us Apart and Makes Us Holy. (Exodus 31:13; Leviticus 20:26)

I. The Lord Is The One Who Makes Us Right With Himself. (Jeremiah 23:6)

J. God Is The One Who Will Pay Back or The Lord Will Punish And Pay Back. (Jeremiah 51:56; Ezekiel 7:9; Romans 12:19)

K. The names that bring all the others together and make them complete are Alpha and Omega. These are the first and last Greek letters and mean the *First and Last*, the *Beginning and End* of all things. These names of God are used in many different parts of God's Word. (Revelation 1:8) One part that uses many of these different names is Psalm 23.

Psalm 23

(1) The Lord is my Shepherd. I will have everything I need. (The Lord is my Shepherd)
(2) He lets me rest in fields of green grass. He leads me beside the quiet waters. (The Lord Who gives me what I want)
(3) He makes me strong again. He leads me in the way of living right with Himself which brings honor to His name. (The Lord Who makes me right with Himself)
(4) Yes, even if I walk through the valley of the shadow of death, I will not be afraid of anything, because You are with me. You have a walking stick with which to guide and one with which to help. These comfort me. (The Lord our peace)
(5) You are making a table of food ready for me in front of those who hate me. You have poured oil on my head. I have everything I need.
(6) For sure, You will give me goodness and loving-kindness all the days of my life. Then I will live with You in Your house forever. (The Lord is here now)

CERTAIN THINGS ABOUT GOD THAT HE DOES NOT SHARE WITH MAN

It is hard to understand the difference between who God is and what God is like. The next two chapters will help to show the difference.

There Are Certain Things About God That He Does Not Share With Man:

1. *GOD ALWAYS WAS AND ALWAYS WILL BE.* Because everything has a beginning and an end, it is hard to understand how God had no beginning. He always was. God is without beginning or end. He is the "I AM." He is always the same. In Revelation 1:8 it says, "The Lord God says, 'I am the First and the Last, the beginning and the end of all things. I am the All-powerful One Who was and Who is and Who is to come.' " And in Psalm 90:2 it says, "Before the mountains were born, before You gave birth to the earth and the world, forever and ever, You are God." (Isaiah 41:4b)

2. *GOD NEVER CHANGES.* Anytime something changes, it is for the better or for the worse. But God cannot change for the better because He is already perfect. He cannot change for the worse because He is God. Malachi 3:6 says, "For I, the Lord, do not change." James 1:17 says, "Whatever is good and perfect comes to us from God. He is the One Who made all light. He does not change. No shadow is made by His turning." (Psalm 33:11)

3. *GOD KNOWS ALL THINGS.* He knows Himself and He knows all other things. He knows everything that will happen to man. He knows if man will put his trust in His Son, or turn away from Him. (Genesis 15:13-15; Exodus 3:7-9; Ecclesiastes 12:14; Luke 12:2; I Corinthians 4:5; I Peter 1:10-12)

   A. God knows what a man is thinking about. I Chronicles 28:9 says, "...For the Lord looks into all hearts, and understands every plan and thought..." No thought can be kept from God. Job 42:2 says, "I know that You can do all things. Nothing can put a stop to Your plans." And in Psalm 139:2 it says, "You know when I sit down and when I get up. You understand my thoughts from far away."

   B. There is not a word that comes from the mouth of man without the Lord knowing it. Psalm 139:4 says, "Even before I speak a word, O Lord, You know it all."

C. We may not think of certain things that we should tell Him, but He knows all things. I John 3:20 says, "Our heart may say that we have done wrong. But remember, God is greater than our heart. He knows everything." "For the ways of a man are seen by the eyes of the Lord, and He watches all his paths" (Proverbs 5:21).

D. The plan God has for man to be saved from the punishment of sin is greater than anything man can think of. In Romans 11:33 it says, "God's riches are so great! The things He knows and His wisdom are so deep. No one can understand His thoughts. No one can understand His ways." (Isaiah 55:7; 64:4; I Corinthians 2:9)

E. God knows each person He has made and knows everything about them. In Matthew 10:29-30 it says, "Are not two small birds sold for a very small piece of money? And yet not one of the birds falls to the earth without your Father knowing it. God knows how many hairs you have on your head." (Psalm 33:13-15; Jeremiah 1:5)

F. God sees all things that happen in every place. In Hebrews 4:13 it says, "No one can hide from God. His eyes see everything we do. We must give an answer to God for what we have done." Proverbs 15:3 says, "The eyes of the Lord are in every place, watching the bad and the good." (Proverbs 5:21)

G. God knows all the sorrows of men. "The Lord said, 'I have seen the suffering of My people in Egypt. I have heard their cry because of the men who make them work. I know how they suffer' " (Exodus 3:7).

H. God knows all things that have happened in the past and all things that will happen in the future. (Isaiah 46:9-10; Acts 2:23; Romans 8:27-29).

Some other verses that show God knows all things:

Acts 1:24 "Then the followers prayed, saying, 'Lord, You know the hearts of all men. Show us which of these two men You have chosen.' " (I Samuel 16:7)

Acts 15:8 "God knows the hearts of all men. He showed them they were to have His loving-favor by giving them the Holy Spirit the same as He gave to us." God knew Pharoah would not let the Israelites go. (Exodus 3:19)

I Corinthians 3:20 "They also say, 'The Lord knows how the wise man thinks. His thinking is worth nothing.' " (Psalm 94:11)

II Timothy 2:19 "But the truth of God cannot be changed. It says, 'The Lord knows those who are His.' And, 'Everyone who says he is a Christian must turn away from sin!' "

Romans 8:29 "God knew from the beginning who would put their trust in Him. So He chose them and made them to be like His Son. Christ was first, and all those who belong to God are His brothers."

4. *GOD IS ALL-POWERFUL.* He can do everything He wants to do. His power has no end. Nothing can change or stop God's power. When God says He will do something, He will do it. (Numbers 23:19)

   A. Men can do *some* things, but they cannot do *all* things. In Matthew 19:26 it says, "Jesus looked at them and said, 'This cannot be done by men. But with God all things can be done.' " (Job 42:2)

   B. God can do things that are hard to believe. Luke 1:36-37 says, "See, your cousin Elizabeth, as old as she is, is going to give birth to a child. She was not able to have children before, but now she is in her sixth month. For God can do all things." (Genesis 18:14)

   C. God does not only give life, but He can also bring a person back to life after death. Acts 26:8 says, "Why do you think it is hard to believe that God raises people from the dead?" John 11:43-44 says, "When He had said this, He called with a loud voice, 'Lazarus, come out!' The man who had been dead came out. His hands and feet were tied in grave clothes. A white cloth was tied around his face. Jesus said to the people, 'Take off the grave clothes and let him go!' " (I Kings 17:22; II Kings 4:32-34; John 11:1-44)

5. *GOD IS EVERYWHERE.* There is no place where God is not. Man must not think of God as having a body like his. Even if man reads of God having ears, eyes, feet, or a right side, it must be understood that this speaks of Him being *able* to see, hear, and feel everywhere at the same time. Man cannot understand how big God is. The heavens are not big enough for Him. II Chronicles 6:18b says, "...See, heaven and the highest heaven cannot hold You. How much less can this house hold You which I have built." Heaven, hell, every part of the sea, all darkness and all light are full of God. And God is not far from each one of those who are His children. Acts 17:27 says, "They were to look for God. Then they might feel after Him

and find Him because He is not far from each one of us." There is no place man can go without God being there. In Jeremiah 23:24 it says, " 'Can a man hide himself in secret places so that I cannot see him?' says the Lord. 'Do I not fill heaven and earth?' says the Lord." God is everywhere because He is Spirit. But there is a special place called heaven where God is. Matthew 5:34-35 tells where God is. "I tell you, do not use strong words when you make a promise. Do not promise by heaven. It is the place where God is. Do not promise by earth. It is where He rests His feet. Do not promise by Jerusalem. It is the city of the great King." While Stephen was being killed, he said in Acts 7:56, "See! I see heaven open and the Son of Man standing at the right side of God!" (Psalm 139:7-10)

CERTAIN THINGS ABOUT GOD THAT HE SHARES WITH MAN

The last chapter taught how God did not share certain things with man. In this chapter it can be seen how God has certain things that He desires to share with man. Man does not have these things himself. After he becomes a Christian and has a desire to live for Him, God shares these things.

1. *GOD IS HOLY.* The word "holy" means to be free from all sin, or to be pure. In I Peter 1:15 it says, "Be holy in every part of your life. Be like the Holy One Who chose you." God is holy and is willing to share this with man. When man is like God in this way, it means he is set apart for God-like living and set apart to work for God. In John 17:11b it says, "Holy Father, keep those You have given to Me in the power of Your name." God speaks of Himself as being holy in I Peter 1:16 when He says, "You must be holy, for I am holy." (Joshua 24:19; Psalm 99:5, 9)

   Luke 1:49 "He Who is powerful has done great things for me. His name is holy." (Isaiah 57:15)

   Revelation 4:8 "Each one of the four living beings had six wings. They had eyes all over them, inside and out. Day and night they never stop saying, 'Holy, holy, holy is the Lord, the All-powerful One. He is the One Who was and Who is and Who is to come.' " (Isaiah 6:3)

   Revelation 6:10 "All those who had been killed cried out with a loud voice saying, 'How long will it be yet before You will punish those on the earth for killing us? Lord, You are holy and true.' " (Deuteronomy 32:43; Psalm 79:10)

   Revelation 15:4 "Who will not honor You, Lord, with love and fear? Who will not tell of the greatness of Your name? For You are the only One Who is holy. All nations will come and worship before You. Everyone sees that You do the right things." (Psalm 86:9; Jeremiah 10:7)

2. *GOD IS ALWAYS RIGHT AND WHATEVER HE DOES IS GOOD.* God made a way for man to be right with Himself. God will forgive and receive the sinner who comes through Jesus' death on the cross. In I Corinthians 1:30 it says, "God Himself made the way so you can have new life through Christ Jesus. God gave us

Christ to be our wisdom. Christ made us right with God, and set us apart for God and made us holy. Christ bought us with His blood and made us free from our sins." (Psalm 19:9; Jeremiah 23:5)

3. *GOD IS ALWAYS FAITHFUL AND TRUE.* God can always be trusted. In I Corinthians 10:13 it tells how God is faithful to His children. "You have never been tempted to sin in any different way than other people. God is faithful. He will not allow you to be tempted more than you can take. But when you are tempted, He will make a way for you to keep from falling into sin." God is faithful in what He promised. In I Thessalonians 5:24 it says, "The One Who called you is faithful and will do what He promised." And in Hebrews 10:23 it says, "Let us hold on to the hope we say we have and not be changed. We can trust God that He will do what He promised." And He is faithful to Himself. In II Timothy 2:13 it says, "If we have no faith, He will still be faithful for He cannot go against what He is." (Deuteronomy 7:9; Isaiah 49:7)

4. *GOD IS A GOD OF LOVING-PITY AND LOVING-KINDNESS.* This is also seen in the Christian who desires to please God. In Romans 2:4 it says, "Do you forget about His loving-kindness to you? Do you forget how long He is waiting for you? You know that God is kind. He is trying to get you to be sorry for your sins and turn from them." In Romans 11:22 it says, "We see how kind God is. It shows how hard He is also. He is hard on those who fall away. But He is kind to you if you keep on trusting Him. If you do not, He will cut you off." (Psalm 89:24)

5. *GOD IS LOVE.* Most people think of God as a God of love. True love is from God and the Christian has love for others because God gives him love. The Christian way of worship is the only way of worship that says God is love. The gods of wood, stone, and other things that many people worship in many parts of the world are thought to be full of hate. These people think something must be given to these false gods all the time so the gods will not punish them. Those who put their trust in God's Son, Jesus Christ, are loved by God. (Deuteronomy 7:7-8; Jeremiah 31:3; II Corinthians 5:14a; 13:11b)

   I John 4:8-16 "Those who do not love do not know God because God is love. God has shown His love to us by sending His only Son into the world. God did this so we might have life through Christ. This is love! It is not that we loved God but that He loved us. For God sent His Son to pay for our sins with His own blood. Dear friends, if God loved us that much, then we should love each other. No person has ever seen God at any time. If we love each other, God lives in us. His love is made perfect in us. He has given us His Spirit.

This is how we know we live by His help and He lives in us. We have seen and are able to say that the Father sent His Son to save the world from the punishment of sin. The person who tells of Him in front of men and says that Jesus is the Son of God, God is living in that one and that one is living by the help of God. We have come to know and believe the love God has for us. God is love. If you live in love, you live by the help of God and God lives in you."

John 14:21 "The one who loves Me is the one who has My teaching and obeys it. My Father will love whoever loves Me. I will love him and will show Myself to him." (Deuteronomy 10:12; Proverbs 8:17)

John 16:27 "...because the Father loves you. He loves you because you love Me and believe that I came from the Father."

John 17:23, 26 "I am in them and You are in Me so they may be one and be made perfect. Then the world may know that You sent Me and that You love them as You love Me." "I have made your name known to them and will make it known. So then the love You have for Me may be in them and I may be in them." God loves the world of men, even though they are sinful. John 3:16 says, "For God so loved the world that He gave His only Son. Whoever puts his trust in God's Son will not be lost, but will have life that lasts forever." Romans 5:8 says, "But God showed His love to us. While we were still sinners, Christ died for us." God took care of the sin problem by giving His Son. (Isaiah 53:5-6)

Romans 1:7 "So I write to all of you in the city of Rome. God loves you and has chosen you to be set apart for Himself. May God our Father and the Lord Jesus Christ give you His loving-favor and peace." (Psalm 91:14)

Romans 5:8 "But God showed His love to us. While we were still sinners, Christ died for us." (Isaiah 53:6)

Galatians 2:20 "I have been put up on the cross to die with Christ. I no longer live. Christ lives in me. The life I now live in this body, I live by putting my trust in the Son of God. He was the One Who loved me and gave Himself for Me."

Ephesians 2:4 "But God had so much loving-kindness. He loved us with such a great love." (Nehemiah 9:17b)

Hebrews 12:6 "The Lord punishes everyone He loves. He whips every son He receives." (Psalm 119:75; Proverbs 3:11-12)

I John 3:1 "See what great love the Father has for us that He would call us His children. And that is what we are. For this reason the people of the world do not know who we are because they did not know Him."

These things God shares with men who have been saved from the punishment of sin, and have a desire to live a God-like life.

WHAT GOD IS LIKE

Since God is Who He is, words are hard to find to tell about Him. The Word of God helps man know about Him and what He is like. It is not possible to tell Who God is without telling what He is like and what He does.

1. *GOD IS SPIRIT.* God does not have a body. Because of Who He is and how He works, He does not need a body like a human being. In John 4:24 it says, "God is Spirit. Those who worship Him must worship Him in Spirit and in truth." (Deuteronomy 4:15; Psalm 139:7)

2. *GOD IS LIGHT.* This tells what He is like and how He works. The first thing He did after He made the world was to make light. "And God said, 'Let there be light,' and there was light" (Genesis 1:3). In I John 1:5 it says, "This is what we heard Him tell us. We are passing it on to you. God is light. There is no darkness in Him." (Isaiah 60:19)

3. *GOD IS LOVE.* God is not only full of love, He is love. He is happy to share His love with man. In I John 4:16 it says, "We have come to know and believe the love God has for us. God is love. If you live in love, you live by the help of God and God lives in you." (God loves man but He hates sin. Proverbs 6:16-19) (Isaiah 43:4; Jeremiah 31:3)

4. *GOD IS A FIRE WHO DESTROYS WHAT IS SINFUL.* God is right in everything He does. He is holy and perfect. When silver and gold are made pure so that no other metal is mixed with them, a hot fire is used to burn away everything that is not good. Fire cleans. In Hebrews 12:29 it says, "For our God is a fire that destroys everything." (Deuteronomy 4:24; 9:3,19)

5. *GOD IS A PERSON.* The three things that make a person are: (1) The power of knowing, (2) The power of feeling, and (3) The power of choosing. God has these three things and He is a person. He does not have a body because He is Spirit. Spirits do not have bodies. We know He is a person because:

   A. *God has the power of knowing.* God knows Himself. When He called Moses from the burning bush, He said, "I AM WHO I AM." It could be said no stronger. God was sure of Himself. God knows all things. In Acts 15:18 it says, "God has made all His works known from the beginning of time." And Hebrews 4:13 says, "No one can hide from God. His eyes see everything we do." (II Chronicles 16:9; Psalm 33:13-15)

B. *God has the power of feeling.* The verse that shows this best is John 3:16, "For God so loved the world..." And James 5:11b says, "The Lord is full of loving-kindness and pity." (Psalm 103:8)

C. *God has the power of choosing.* Psalm 115:3 says, "But our God is in the heavens. He does whatever He wants to do." (Psalm 103:19)

6. *GOD DOES NOT CHANGE.* Nothing can change Him or His actions. He has no beginning and He will always be. God always has been the same and always will be the same. In Malachi 3:6a it says, "For I, the Lord, do not change." It also says in James 1:17a, "Whatever is good and perfect comes to us from God. He is the One Who made all light. He does not change." Hebrews 6:17-18 says, "And so God made a promise. He wanted to show Abraham that He would never change His mind. So He made the promise in His own name. God gave these two things that cannot be changed and God cannot lie. We who have turned to Him can have great comfort knowing that He will do what He has promised." (I Samuel 15:29)

7. *GOD IS ALL WISDOM.* God is not only wise, but He knows all things. He uses what He knows in a way that is right and good. In Romans 11:33 it says, "God's riches are so great! The things He knows and His wisdom are so deep! No one can understand His thoughts. No one can understand His ways." (Psalm 104:24; Daniel 2:20)

8. *GOD IS ALL-POWERFUL.* There is nothing God cannot do. Matthew 19:26 says, "But with God all things can be done." (Jeremiah 32:17)

9. *GOD IS HOLY AND PERFECT.* Everything He does is right and good. In I Peter 1:15-16 it says, "Be holy in every part of your life. Be like the Holy One Who chose you. The Holy Writings say, 'You must be holy, for I am holy.' " Also in John 17:11 it says, "I am no longer in the world. I am coming to you. But these are still in the world. Holy Father, keep those You have given to Me in the power of Your Name. Then they will be one, even as We are One." (Deuteronomy 32:4; Psalm 18:30a)

10. *GOD IS TRUTH.* In John 3:33 it says, "Whoever receives His words proves that God is true." Part of Romans 3:4 says, "God is

always true even if every man lies." I John 5:6-7 says, "Jesus Christ came by water and blood. He did not come by water only, but by water and blood. The Holy Spirit speaks about this and He is truth. There are three who speak of this in heaven: the Father and the Word and the Holy Spirit. These three are one." (Isaiah 65:16)

11. *GOD IS THE ONE WHO BRINGS EVERYTHING INTO BEING, KEEPS IT, AND BRINGS IT TO ITS END.* Everything is under God's great power, and He is the One Who is head over all things. In Isaiah 45:5-7 it says, "I am the Lord, and there is no other. There is no God besides Me. I will give you strength, even though you have not known me. Then men may know from sunrise to sunset that there is no God besides Me. I am the Lord, and there is no other. I make the light, and I make darkness. I bring good and I make trouble. I am the Lord Who does all these things." Colossians 1:17b says, "All things are held together by Him."

12. *GOD IS THREE-IN-ONE.* (See the next chapter for this study.)

THE THREE-IN-ONE GOD

The Three-in-one God or *Trinity* means that there is one God in three persons as: Father, Son, and Holy Spirit. This is hard to understand, and yet the Word of God tells of one God in three persons. This may help. A large group of people meeting together is called *one* group. Some grapes grow together and are called *one bunch*. The husband and wife are *one*. Matthew 19:5 says, "For this reason a man will leave his father and his mother and will live with his wife. The two will become *one*."

Matthew 3:16-17 shows the three different persons. "When Jesus came out of the water, the heavens opened. He saw the Spirit of God coming down and resting on Jesus like a dove. A voice was heard from heaven. It said, 'This is My much-loved Son. I am very happy with Him.' " The *Father* speaks from heaven, the *Son* is baptized in the Jordan River, and the *Holy Spirit* comes down on the Son as a dove. In Matthew 28:19 Jesus tells His followers to baptize new Christians in the name of the Father, and the Son, and the Holy Spirit.

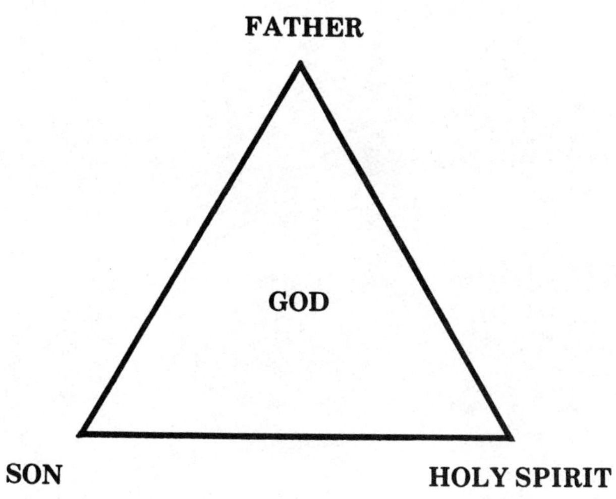

GOD IS ONE GOD IN THREE PERSONS.

Paul ends his letter to the Christians in the city of Corinth by saying in II Corinthians 13:14, "May you have loving-favor from our Lord Jesus Christ. May you have the love of God. May you be joined together by the Holy Spirit."

In John 14:16a Jesus says, "Then I will ask My Father and He will give you another helper." *Jesus* is asking the *Father* to give the *Holy Spirit*. In Romans 1:7 it speaks of the *Father* Who is God; in Hebrews 1:8 the *Son* Who is God; and in Acts 5:3-4 the *Holy Spirit* Who is God. Not one of the three Persons is greater or less than the others, and there can never be a division among them.

It may help to understand by thinking of it this way:

The Father is God, the part of the Three-in-one God Who is not seen. (John 1:18) The Son is God, the part of the Three-in-one God Who left heaven to live in human flesh among sinful men. (John 1:14-18) The Holy Spirit is God, the part of the Three-in-one God Who works in and through men. (I Corinthians 2:9-10)

THE WORKS OF GOD

The works of God are what He has done in the past, what He is doing now, and what He will do in the future. In Romans 1:20 it says, "Men cannot say they do not know about God. From the beginning of the world, men could see what God is like through the things He has made. This shows His power that lasts forever. It shows that He is God." They see His works. But to know His works is not the same as knowing His ways. His works may be known by those who know about Him. But His ways are known by those who know Him as a person. "He made known His ways to Moses, and His acts (works) to the children of Israel." The works of God show His plan for all times. In I Timothy 1:17 it says, "We give honor and thanks to the King Who lives forever. He is the One Who never dies and Who is never seen. He is the One Who knows all things. He is the only God. Let it be so." In Ephesians 1:11 it says, "We were already chosen to be God's own children by Christ. This was done just like the plan He had." It can be seen how everything works as He planned it. God works just as He plans. This is seen in Ephesians 3:11, "This was the plan God had for all time. He did this through Christ Jesus our Lord."

1. *GOD MADE [BROUGHT INTO BEING] EVERYTHING.*

The word *creation* is used in most versions. It means the work of the Three-in-one God by which in the beginning and for His own shining greatness, He made, without the use of anything that was before, the whole world that can be seen and that which cannot be seen. (Genesis 1:1-2; John 1:1-3)

2. *IT CAN BE SEEN THAT EVERY WORK OF GOD IS DONE BY THE THREE-IN-ONE GOD.*

A. God the Father was the One Who planned it and started it. Ephesians 3:9 says, "I was to make all men understand the meaning of this secret. God kept this secret to Himself from the beginning of the world. And He is the One Who made all things." (Genesis 1:1; Deuteronomy 4:39; I Corinthians 8:6; II Corinthians 4:6)

B. God the Son brought it into being. Colossians 1:16 says, "Christ made everything in the heavens and on the earth. He made everything that is seen and things that are not seen. He made all the powers of heaven. Everything was made by Him and for Him." (John 1:1-3; I Corinthians 8:6; Hebrews 1:2; 11:3)

C. God the Holy Spirit finished it. (Genesis 1:2; Job 26:13; 33:4)

It can be thought of this way: When a house is built, one plans how it is to be built. Another builds the building, and another finishes the inside. Each had a part. This can be seen in Genesis 1:1-3: God the Father in verse 1, God the Spirit in verse 2, and God the Son in verse 3. God did not only make the world that is seen, He made things that are not seen. He made the angel world as seen in Colossians 1:16, which says, "Christ made everything in the heavens and on earth. He made everything that is seen and things that are not seen. He made all the powers of heaven. Everything was made by Him and for Him."

The Hebrew word for *created* is found three times in Genesis 1. In verse 1 - God *created* (made from nothing) the heavens and the earth. In verse 21 - He made animal life. In verse 26 - He made human life. Man has always had a desire to know how God did these things, but He chose to keep His ways a secret. Some people make the mistake of thinking the things God made are God Himself. God should not be worshiped in what He has made. These things prove that an All-powerful God made them, but men must not worship them. Man must worship the One Who made them. The question is asked, why did God *create* (make things from nothing)? There is only one answer. God made everything for His own shining greatness, just as He wanted them, and for His own use. This is seen in Revelation 4:11, "Our Lord and our God, it is right for you to have the shining greatness and the honor and power. You made all things. They were made and have life because you wanted it that way." (Nehemiah 9:6; Romans 11:36; Ephesians 1:5)

3. GOD KEEPS AND TAKES CARE OF THINGS HE MADE.

Colossians 1:17 says, "Christ was before all things. All things are held together by Him." Some people have made the mistake of thinking God has left the world to run by itself. Hebrews 1:3 says, "The Son shines with the shining greatness of the Father. The Son is as God is in every way. It is the Son Who holds up the whole world by the power of His Word. The Son gave His own life so we could be clean from all sin. After He had done that He sat down on the right side of God in heaven." This is the part Christ has in keeping things together and running well. Christ spoke of the birds of the sky and the flowers of the field as being cared for by God. If He cares for them, how much more does He care for man? (Matthew 5:45; 6:26; 10:29-31)

God shows in His Word that He has made and is keeping things as He wants them.

A. The earth, sun, moon, and stars stay as they were planned. (Psalm 119:89-91)

B. The nations of the world are where God put them or where He allows them to be. Acts 17:26 says, "He made from one blood all nations who live on the earth. He set the times and places where they should live." (Deuteronomy 32:8)

C. The length of human life is as God planned it. Job 14:5 says, "A man's days are numbered. You know the number of his months. He cannot live longer than the time You have set."

D. The acts of man, both good and bad, are allowed by God. Luke 22:22 says, "The Son of Man will be taken this way because it has been in God's plan. But it is bad for that man who hands Him over!" (Acts 2:23; 4:27-28; Ephesians 2:10; I Peter 2:8; Revelation 17:17)

E. The saving of men from the punishment of sin is by God's plan. (Isaiah 53:5; Romans 8:29-30; Ephesians 1:3, 10, 11)

PART 2

WHAT THE WORD OF GOD TEACHES ABOUT ITSELF

[*Bibliology*]

THE HOLY WRITINGS

1. THE HOLY WRITINGS CAME FROM GOD.

The Bible is the only written word God has for people. This greatest of all books *The Holy Bible* does not just have God's Word in it, it *IS* the Word of God. It is all of the Holy Writings of God in one Book. There are sixty-six different books in the Bible. Thirty-nine of these are in the Old Testament and twenty-seven are in the New Testament.

God used about 40 different men to write what He told them to write. The first books were written about 1,500 years before Christ and the last ones were written about 100 years after Christ's death. From the beginning to the end it was 1,600 years. II Peter 1:20-21 says, "Understand this first: No part of the Holy Writings was ever made up by man. No part of the Holy Writings came long ago because of what man wanted to write. But holy men who belonged to God spoke what the Holy Spirit told them."

The Holy Writings were written long ago. And yet they were written for all people and for all times. There has been no need for other writings to be given from God after the first ones because they were complete. God's Word has everything a person needs to know about God, about Jesus Christ, about the Holy Spirit, about the way for a sinful person to become a child of God, about how to have peace in this life, and about life after death. God has given us His Word in writing. It can never be destroyed. Matthew 24:35 says, "Heaven and earth will pass away, but My words will not pass away."

2. THE HOLY WRITINGS ARE IN TWO PARTS - THE OLD TESTAMENT AND THE NEW TESTAMENT.

The word *Testament* means that God agreed or promised to do certain things for His people. Later, this word came to mean the book which had these promises in it.

God has always wanted people to worship Him. The Old Testament can be called the *Old Way of Worship*. It is the same with the New Testament. It can be called the *New Way of Worship* because the two ways of worship are different. The first, or Old Way of Worship, was by a set of laws or rules and the giving of animals or other things on the altar as an act of worship. In the New Way of Worship, Christ was given. He was God's perfect gift. Christ was the only one Who was able to keep the old laws. When man puts his trust in Christ, he gives God his true worship. (Hebrews 9:1-14)

A. *The Old Testament* tells of the beginning of the world and all that God made on it and around it. It tells how He gave His laws or rules for living to His people. It tells how men lived in that day. Sometimes they pleased God and sometimes they fought against Him. It tells how certain men were able to tell what would happen in the future. And it tells how Christ, the Promised One, the Son of God, would come to save people from the punishment of their sins when they put their trust in Him.

B. *The New Testament* tells of the birth, life, and death of Christ, and this happened as it was told it would happen in the Old Testament by God's early preachers. It tells of the beginning of the church as it is known today. It tells of the problems of the new churches and what must be done to live in a way to please God. It tells what will happen before Christ comes to earth the second time and how it will happen.

3. *THE BIBLE IS* **THE** *BOOK.*

The English word *Bible* comes from the language in which the New Testament was written. Bible means *book.* About 500 years after the birth of Christ, the Holy Books came to be called *The Holy Bible.*

Sometimes the writings in the Bible are called the Scriptures which means the *Holy Writings.* The first Christians called the Word of God *The Scriptures.*

The Bible is not just a book. It is **THE** Book. It is the most important of all books because of the One Who caused It to be written, and what It has in It. The word *Holy* is in front of the word *Bible* and is used because the Word of God is truth and It is set apart from all other books as God's Word to people of all times.

Long ago God chose certain men to write down what He told them. There were many different men. They lived at different times and at different places. Their lives were different because of the places where they lived. Many of them never saw each other. Their families were different. God used men as men, not as *machines.* The writings that were written down all agree with each other and show that they came from the same Person. That Person was God.

HOW THE BIBLE CAME TO MAN

1. THE BIBLE CAME TO MAN IN A POWERFUL WAY.

God has kept His Writings over the many years. The Old Testament was written in the Hebrew language on animal skins. This was the way it was kept until books were printed. The New Testament books were written in the Greek language on writing paper made from *papyrus reed* that grew in Egypt. For many years the words of the Bible were written one word at a time by hand. The first Bible to be put into the English language was in the year 1382. The first Bible to be printed was in 1454. The King James Bible was *translated* from the Greek and Hebrew languages into the English language and printed in the year 1611. The Word of God has been put into many different languages so people over all the world can understand it. This was why The NEW LIFE Testament was put into easy-to-read English. In this way God's Word can mean even more because it is easy to read and understand.

NEW LIFE
Testament 1969
Bible 1986

Many other
Translations
from
1900-1970

Wycliffe
Bible
1320

First
Writings
in
Greek
&
Hebrew

Berkeley
Bible
1959

Tyndale
Bible
1525

Amplified
Bible
1958

King James
Bible
1611

Revised
Standard
Bible
1952

2. THERE ARE FALSE WRITINGS THAT SINFUL MEN TRY TO SAY ARE THE WORD OF GOD.

There are some writings that people have wanted to put in the Bible that are not God's Word. These false writings must not be taken for God's Word.

About 1,500 years ago the leaders of the church met to take a careful look at these books and test them for the truth. There are many false books that have been written that look like the Holy Writings. These false writings have words in them that talk about God, but they were not written by holy men God spoke through. The Holy Writings must not be added to or have words taken from them. Deuteronomy 4:2 says, "Do not add to the Word that I tell you, and do not take away from it. Keep the Laws of the Lord your God which I tell you." Revelation 22:18-19 says, "I am telling everyone who hears the words that are written in this book: If anyone adds anything to what is written in this book, God will add to him the kinds of trouble that this book tells about. If anyone takes away any part of this book that tells what will happen in the future, God will take away his part from the tree of life and from the Holy City which are written in this book."

3. *HOW IT WAS DECIDED WHICH WRITINGS WERE GOD-GIVEN AND MADE ALIVE BY HIM.*

There were certain men God chose to write His word. But there were other men who wrote other writings that looked much like God's Word, and some even tried to call these false writings *Holy* writings. Books that became part of the Bible had to pass certain tests.

A. The books in the Old Testament had to be written, put together, or spoken of as true, by an early preacher. The Writings in the New Testament had to be written by one of the twelve men Christ chose to follow Him, or one who lived and worked with one of the followers of these men.

B. Help had to come from these Writings so that people could grow in their Christian lives.

C. The Writings had to be already in use by the churches and had to have proved themselves.

D. The most important test was if the book showed that it was God-given and made alive by Him.

Every one of the 66 books in the Bible today have gone through many tests. The 66 books that are in the Bible passed the tests. The other writings that did not pass these same tests are not put - and should not be put - in the Bible.

WHY THE BIBLE WAS WRITTEN

1. *THE MOST IMPORTANT REASON FOR THE THE BIBLE BEING WRITTEN WAS FOR GOD TO TELL PEOPLE THE THINGS HE WANTED THEM TO KNOW. THE BIBLE IS GOD SPEAKING.*

   A. God spoke in the Old Testament through special preachers who wrote down what He told them. Hebrews 1:1 says, "Long ago God spoke to our early fathers in many and different ways. He spoke through the early preachers." (Luke 1:70; Acts 3:21; Romans 1:2) In the Old Testament He tells how the world and everything in it was made and how He helped His people, the Jews. The Old Testament also tells the news that He would send His Son, Jesus, at a later time. (Jeremiah 36:2-3; Ezekiel 1:3)

   B. God spoke in the New Testament through Jesus. In Hebrews 1:2a it says, "But in these last days He (God) has spoken to us through His Son."

      The New Testament tells about the birth of Jesus and His work while on earth. God's Word says many things about people also. God wants man to know he is a sinner. Then God wants him to know what can be done to be saved from the punishment of sin. In Romans 6:20-23 it says, "When sin had power over your life, you were not right with God. What good did you get from the things you are ashamed of now? Those things bring death. But now you are free from the power of sin. You have become a servant for God. Your life is set apart for God-like living. The end is life that lasts forever. You get what is coming to you when you sin. It is death! But God's free gift is life that lasts forever. It is given to us by our Lord Jesus Christ."

      Once a man sees this truth and puts his trust in Christ, he finds the Bible has much in it to help him live his life in the right way. In II Timothy 3:16-17 it says, "All the Holy Writings are God-given and are made alive by Him. Man is helped when he is taught God's Word. It shows what is wrong. It changes the way of a man's life. It shows him how to be right with God. It gives the man who belongs to God everything he needs to work well for Him."

      When a man wonders what the answer is to problems he has in his life, he should read the Word of God. Great comfort can be found in God's Word, and it tells everything man needs to know to live for God.

2. *THE BIBLE WAS WRITTEN FOR MAN TO LEARN ABOUT GOD.*

Christians can learn something by reading the Bible again and again. The Holy Spirit helps man understand what God is saying to him through the Bible. The Bible will help Christians grow to become stronger Christians. It is hard for a man to read a book when the room is getting dark. It is hard to see what he is reading. When he turns on a light, it becomes easy to read. The same is true when the Bible seems hard to understand. When he asks the Holy Spirit to help him, it is like a light to his mind making it easier for him to know what he is reading.

The Bible is not God, but it is God speaking. God has spoken and the Bible is His Word in writing to man. II Peter 1:20-21 says, "No part of the Holy Writings was ever made up by any man. No part of the Holy Writings came long ago because of what man wanted to write. But holy men who belonged to God spoke (wrote) what the Holy Spirit told them."

THE HOLY WRITINGS ARE GOD-GIVEN AND MADE ALIVE BY HIM

How the Holy Writings were given is hard to understand. No one knows all the answers.

1. GOD GAVE HIS WORD TO MEN TO WRITE.

At different times during 1,600 years 40 different men were used of God to write the sixty-six books of the Bible, yet it is only one Book. It tells of the one and only way to be saved from sin, and the one way to heaven. No other religious book has such a plan. No other book has proven all it contains is true.

How the Holy Writings were given is hard to understand. A special power that is not known today was given to the holy men long ago who wrote down what God led them to write even to the very words they should use. They were kept from making a mistake and from leaving out anything that should have been written. It was power given by the Holy Spirit but we do not know how it worked. This power was given only to the men who wrote the Holy Writings. This means that no other books are God's Holy Writings. The Holy Spirit *led* or *guided* them in what they wrote and the words to use. This means that the first writings had no mistakes. (It is possible for Bibles written in the languages of today to have mistakes. Words in any language change in meaning over many years, and because of this some of the meanings are not the same today. It is important that people be sure the Bible they read is true to the languages the Bible was first written in.)

2. GOD GAVE HIS WORD TO MAN.

God is powerful, holy, pure, and full of love, and has loving-pity for the people He made. It can be seen everywhere that He has made things for man to use. He gives air to breathe. He makes the seeds grow and gives sunshine and rain. He has given man the understanding as to how to make these things give him what he needs. But man needs more than just these things. He has a sin problem! He feels guilty and knows something is wrong in his heart. None of the things that God made for man to use, or the understanding a man has can help him know what to do about the guilty feeling, or how to be right with God. Man knows there is something more after this life. He needs to be ready for life after death. God who gave man all the other things he needed, also made a way for him to know and understand how he can be right with God. He gave man His holy pure Word.

3. GOD'S WORD IS TO BE TRUSTED.

A. The Bible, God's Word, is more important than any other religious book. It tells what man must be like to be right with God. It tells how bad sin is and tells the sinner how to get right with God.

B. Two different times God's Word tells of the very words being written by God and Christ. In Exodus 31:18 it says, "When the Lord had finished speaking with Moses on Mount Sinai, He gave him the two stone writings of the Law, pieces of stone written on by the finger of God." And in John 8:6 it says, "Jesus got down and began to write in the dust with His finger." Both of these writings were soon destroyed. The pieces of stone with the written Law were broken in front of the children of Israel who were worshiping a false god, and it was not long before the people walked over what Jesus had written on the ground. But it pleased God to have His Law and the Good News of life that lasts forever written through men He chose for that special job.

C. It is important to know that Jesus trusted and taught the Old Testament Writings. Never once did He tell His followers they needed to watch out for mistakes in the Holy Writings. Jesus was quick to show the wrong-doings of the people of His day. (Matthew 23) In Luke 9:55 it says, "Jesus turned and spoke sharp words to them. He said, 'You do not know what kind of spirit you have. The Son of Man did not come to destroy men's lives. He came to save them from the punishment of sin.' " It was easy for Him to get them straight in their thinking about things so it would have been just as easy for Him to tell about certain mistakes that got into the early Holy Writings which were not given by His Spirit, if there had been any.

But instead of this, He always used the Holy Writings, making it plain to the people that every word could be trusted. Matthew 5:18 says, "I tell you, as long as heaven and earth last, not one small mark or part of a word will pass away of the Law of Moses until it has all been done." And in Luke 21:22 it says, "All things will happen as it is written." In Luke 24:44 it says, "All things written about Me in the Law of Moses and in the Books of the early preachers and in the Psalms must happen as they said they would happen." Jesus used the words *The Law of Moses and the Books of the early preachers and the Psalms* when speaking of the whole Old Testament. Such words would not be used by Jesus if any parts were not given by the Holy Spirit or were not true.

4. THE BIBLE IS GOD'S WORD - NOT MAN'S WORD.

And so, the Holy Writings were written by men God chose for that job. God's written Word was breathed upon and made alive by Him. As time went on, other men put these same words on other skins and on *papyrus reed* paper. The first ones were destroyed or lost. Some of the ones made later are in some of the large cities of the world and can be read by those who know the languages in which they were written. We still have with us today about 1,000 pieces of the Old Testament and about 4,000 pieces of the New Testament.

GOD'S WORD IS TRUE

1. *THE BIBLE IS TRUE BECAUSE GOD SAYS IT IS TRUE.*

The Bible is God's Word. God always tells the truth. So the Bible is true because it is God's Word. Psalm 119:89 says, "Forever, O Lord, Your Word will never change in heaven." Psalm 119:160 says, "All of Your Word is truth, and every one of Your laws, which are always right, will last forever." Isaiah 40:8 says, "The grass dries up. The flower loses its color. But the Word of our God stands forever."

2. *THE BIBLE IS TRUE BECAUSE JESUS BELIEVED IT TO BE TRUE.*

Jesus knew the Holy Writings, now called the Old Testament. He loved them, lived by them, preached them, built His teachings on them, called them *the Truth, God's Truth, and God's Word.* In Luke 4:4-12 when Jesus was tempted by the devil, He spoke words from the Holy Writings. In Luke 4:16-21 it says that Jesus read the Holy Writings at Nazareth. When praying to God the Father, Jesus said in John 17:17b, "Your Word is truth." Jesus says in Matthew 24:35, "Heaven and earth will pass away, but My words will not pass away."

Jesus said in John 10:35, "The Word of God cannot be put aside." Jesus taught from the Holy Writings because He believed them. These are some of the things Jesus believed happened that are told about in the Holy Writings:

A. God made man (Genesis 2:7; Matthew 19:4)

B. Marriage (Genesis 2:24; Matthew 19:5)

C. The burning bush (Exodus 3:4-6; Luke 20:37)

D. Moses (Exodus 20:1-21; Deuteronomy 25:5; Mark 7:10; 12:19-26)

E. The blood of Abel (Genesis 4:8; Luke 11:51)

F. Noah and the flood (Genesis 6:5-7; Matthew 24:37-39)

G. Solomon and the Queen of Sheba (I Kings 10:1; Matthew 12:42)

H. Abraham, Isaac, Jacob (Exodus 3:6; Mark 12:26)

I. Lot, his wife, and the city of Sodom were destroyed (Genesis 19; Luke 17:28, 29, 32)

J. The food God sent from heaven to the people in the desert (Exodus 16:4-5; John 6:31, 32, 49)

K. The snake on a pole (Numbers 21:9; John 3:14)

L. Elijah and the long time everyone was without food. The woman whose husband had died at Zarepath. Naaman healed from a very bad skin disease. (I Kings 17:1-9; II Kings 5:1-14; Luke 4:25-27)

M. Jonah in the fish (Jonah 1:17; Matthew 12:39-41; 16:4)

Jesus began His time of preaching on earth with the words, "It is written." (Matthew 4:4, 7, 10) "Jesus said, 'You foolish men. How slow you are to believe what the early preachers have said' " (Luke 24:25).

Jesus taught using words from 22 books of the Old Testament. He taught from the Holy Writings as Words from God. Not once did He take away from the words and from the truth of them. He said that He did not come to do away with the Law of Moses or the Writings of the early preachers. "I have not come to do away with them but to complete them. I tell you, as long as heaven and earth last, not one small mark or part of a word will pass away of the Law of Moses until it has all been done" (Matthew 5:17-18). Jesus knew that even the smallest letter used in writing God's Word was important.

3. *THE BIBLE IS TRUE BECAUSE THE WRITERS OF THE NEW TESTAMENT BELIEVED GOD'S WORD TO BE TRUE.*

In Matthew there are about 55 verses used from the Old Testament

Mark	32	
Luke	40	
John	30	
Acts	40	
Romans	55	
Corinthians	15	
II Corinthians	8	
Galatians	12	
Ephesians	5	
I Timothy	1	
II Timothy	1	
Hebrews	35 →	(16 Old Testament books are used in Hebrews. Many of them are used a number of times.)
James	4	
I Peter	9	
II Peter	2	
Jude	1	

4. *THE BIBLE IS TRUE BECAUSE MANY OF THE THINGS IT SAID WOULD HAPPEN HAVE ALREADY HAPPENED.*

A. Things happened in the life of Jesus that the Bible told about many years before Jesus was born.

Number of years before Jesus' birth	Where it is found in the Old Testament	Where it happened in the New Testament in the life of Jesus	
1898 yrs.	Gen. 18:18	Born in Abraham's family	Acts 3:25
1898 yrs.	Gen. 17:19	Born in Isaac's family	Matt. 1:2
1452 yrs.	Num. 24:17	Born in Jacob's family	Luke 3:34
1689 yrs.	Gen. 49:10	Born in Judah's family	Luke 3:33
710 yrs.	Micah 5:2	Place of birth	Matt. 2:1
538 yrs.	Daniel 9:25	Time of birth	Luke 2:1-2
742 yrs.	Isaiah 7:14	Born of a woman who had never had a man	Matt. 1:18
487 yrs.	Zech. 11:12	Sold for 30 pieces of silver	Matt.26:15
712 yrs.	Isaiah 53:12	On the cross beside sinners	Matt.27:38
1050 yrs.	Psalm 109:4	Prays for enemies	Luke 23:34
1050 yrs.	Psalm 34:20	Not a bone broken	John 19:33,36
1050 yrs.	Psalm 16:10	Raised from the dead	Matt.28:9

B. God's Word also tells many things about the Jewish nation. Things that were told many years ago have come true.

5. *THE BIBLE IS TRUE BECAUSE THE WAY IT WAS WRITTEN SHOWS IT IS THE WORD OF GOD.*

Most of the men who wrote the books of the Bible had never seen each other. Some of the men even spoke different languages and lived in different countries. Some of the men were shepherds. Some were kings. One made tents. One was a doctor and one was a tax-collector. Yet every part of the Bible agrees with all other parts. Only the All-powerful God could have led all these men to write one Book.

6. *THE BIBLE IS TRUE BECAUSE OF THE WAY IT CHANGES LIVES.*

No other book has done the things the Bible has done. The Bible tells of the only way for man to have peace with God. It tells how man must be born again. God's great power can be seen changing lives when people read and obey what the Bible teaches. The Bible tells how man can come to God. Jesus says that He is the *Way* and the

Truth and the *Life*. He says that no one can go to the Father except by Him. (John 14:6)

7. *THE BIBLE IS TRUE BECAUSE TRUTH NEVER CHANGES.*

Books that have been written by men lose their meaning as the years go by. The Bible still has meaning and truth to all who read it today just as much as it did for those who first read it years ago.

8. *THE BIBLE IS TRUE BECAUSE IT HAS NEVER BEEN OR NEVER CAN BE DESTROYED.*

Some men have tried to destroy the Bible. Some men tried to burn all the copies of the Bible. People have been put to death with much pain for having a Bible. But the more men try to destroy the Bible, the more it is read and believed.

PART 3

WHAT THE WORD OF GOD TEACHES ABOUT CHRIST

[*Christology*]

CHRIST IS ONE OF THE THREE-IN-ONE GOD

1. *CHRIST ALWAYS WAS, IS NOW, AND ALWAYS WILL BE.*

The Word of God tells in many places that Christ was with the Father. There has never been a time when Christ was not. The first five verses in John tell of this. John 1:1-5 says, "The Word (Christ) was in the beginning. The Word was with God. The Word was God. He was with God in the beginning. He made all things. Nothing was made without Him making it. Life began by Him. His Life was the Light for men. The Light shines in the darkness. The darkness has never been able to put out the Light." The first verse of Genesis tells about when the world was made. But John tells us about the One Who was before the world was made. As there has never been a time when God the Father was not, so there has never been a time when Christ was not.

Some *translations* of the New Testament use the word *begotten* in John 3:16. This word in the English language means *brought into the world* or *given life* which would mean that Christ was not with the Father from the beginning, but began life in Bethlehem. The Greek word means *only* or *only one of a kind.*

In Philippians 2:6-7 it says, "Jesus has always been as God is. But He did not hold to His rights as God. He put aside everything that belonged to Him and made Himself the same as a servant who is owned by someone. He became human by being born as a man." Christ was with the Father before He came as a man to live among men. Certain things belong only to God. When Christ left heaven to come to this world, He (as God) did not lay these things aside, but He did not use them while He was on earth.

Hebrews 1:2-3 says, "But in these last days He has spoken to us through His Son. God gave His Son everything. It was by His Son that God made the world. The Son shines with the shining greatness of the Father. The Son is as God is in every way. It is the Son Who holds up the whole world by the power of His Word. The Son gave His own life so we could be clean from all sin. After He had done that, He sat down on the right side of God in Heaven." Christ brought the world into being and keeps it by His power. In Colossians 1:16 it says that all things are for Christ and by Him. Hebrews 10:5-7 tells why Christ came to earth. "When Christ came to the world, He said to God, 'You do not want animals killed or gifts given in worship. You have made My body ready to give as a gift. You are not pleased with animals that have been killed or burned and given as gifts on the altar to take away sin.' Then I said, 'I have come to do what You want, O God. It is written in the Law that I would.' "

Jesus said in John 8:58 that He was before Abraham. In John 17:5 He spoke of the shining greatness which He had with the Father before the world was. In John 17:24 He spoke of the Father's love for Him before the world was made. When Jesus talked with His followers in the room on the second floor before He gave His life, He said, "I came from the Father and have come into the world. I am leaving the world and going to the Father." Christ was before John the Baptist (John 1:15); before Abraham (John 8:58); and before the world was made. (John 1:1; 17:5, 24; Colossians 1:17; Hebrews 1:2)

Christ is One of the Three-in-one God. He is the One Who left heaven and lived in human flesh. I Timothy 3:16 says, "It is important to know the secret of God-like living, which is: Christ came to earth as a Man. He was pure in His spirit. He was seen by angels. The nations heard about Him. Men everywhere put their trust in Him. He was taken up into heaven." (Christ was the Lamb of God Who was killed for man like a lamb and given on the altar.) A good man who was full of loving-pity and loving-kindness would not have been good enough. Man needed the Lord of heaven, the Christ Who could pay for man's sins with His own blood and set him free. Man needed One Who has always been alive and always will be. (Isaiah 53:6)

Making the world from nothing was the work of Christ. John 1:3 says, "He made all things. Nothing was made without Him making it." Colossians 1:16 says, "Christ made everything in the heavens and on the earth. He made everything that is seen and things that are not seen. He made all the powers of heaven. Everything was made by Him and for Him." In Colossians 1:15 it says, "Christ is as God is. God cannot be seen. Christ lived before everything was made." It is true that He entered the human family to live as a man, but this was not the beginning of life for Him. He always was. All things were made by Christ and for Him. Nothing was made that He did not make. That is why Christ is the Head of all things.

2. *CHRIST IS SEEN IN THE OLD TESTAMENT.* He showed Himself in two ways:

   A. In the Old Testament, Christ is seen in things or objects. Some of the things that Christ is seen in were in the Garden of Eden. Adam and Eve were allowed to see the shining greatness of the Lord and hear the voice of the LORD God. "Then they heard the sound of the Lord God walking in the garden in the evening. The man and his wife hid themselves from the Lord God among the trees of the garden" (Genesis 3:8). After sin entered into the hearts of the first two people, special cherubim stood east of the garden of Eden holding burning swords. "So He drove the man out. And He placed cherubim east of the garden of Eden with a sword of fire that turned every way. They kept watch over the path to the tree of life" (Genesis 3:24). These were the ones through which Christ made Himself known at that time. He showed Himself to Abraham before he moved to the land of Canaan. "Now the Lord said to Abram, 'Leave your country, your family and your father's house, and go to the land that I will show you. And I will make you a great nation. I will bring good to you. I will make your name great, so you will be honored. I will bring good to those who are good to you. And I will curse those who curse you. Good will come to all the families of the earth because of you' " (Genesis 12:1-3).

At the burning bush, Moses saw the fire and heard the voice of God. "Now Moses was taking care of the flock of his father-in-law Jethro, the religious leader of Midian. He led the flock to the west side of the desert, and came to Horeb, the mountain of God. There the Angel of the Lord showed Himself to Moses in a burning fire from inside a bush. Moses looked and saw that the bush was burning with fire, but it was not being burned up. So Moses said, 'I must step aside and see this great thing, why the bush is not being burned up.' The Lord saw him step aside to look. And God called to him from inside the bush, saying, 'Moses, Moses!' Moses answered, 'Here I am.' God said, 'Do not come near. Take your shoes off your feet. For the place where you are standing is holy ground.' He said also, 'I am the God of your father, the God of Abraham, the God of Isaac, and the God of Jacob.' Then Moses hid his face. For he was afraid to look at God" (Exodus 3:1-6).

God was able to lead the Jewish people with a cloud during the day and with a fire during the night. "The Lord went before them, in a pillar of cloud during the day to lead them on the way, and in a pillar of fire during the night to give them light. So they could travel day and night. The pillar of cloud during the day and the pillar of fire during the night did not leave the people" (Exodus 13:21-22). The shining greatness of God was seen when a cloud covered the place of worship. "Then the cloud covered the meeting tent. The shining greatness of the Lord filled the holy tent. Moses was not able to go into the meeting tent because the cloud had rested upon it and the shining greatness of the Lord filled the holy tent. When the cloud was lifted from the meeting tent, the people of Israel would go on their way through all their traveling days. But when the cloud was not lifted, they did not move on until the day when it was lifted. For the cloud of the Lord rested on the meeting tent during the day. And fire was in the cloud during the night. It was seen by all the house of Israel as they traveled" (Exodus 40:34-38).

It is in these things or objects that Christ was seen by the people in the Old Testament times. *The shining greatness of the Lord* is a name for Christ as He was *seen* by men. *The Word of the Lord* is a name for Christ as He was *heard* by men.

B. In the Old Testament, Christ is seen as a person. There is a being called the Angel of Jehovah. He has the right and the power to do things that others cannot or must not do. He has the right to be worshiped. The Bible speaks of One such Being or Angel. This One is also called the Son of God and the All-powerful God.

The work done by this Angel of Jehovah is said to be the work of Christ Himself. (Genesis 22:1, 11, 12, 16;32:24-32)

In Micah 5:2 it teaches that Christ showed Himself many times in the early days. These times when He was seen and heard in the Old Testament were as pictures of when He would come to earth in human flesh. His birth in the town of Bethlehem was not the beginning of Him, because He always was.

Each One of the Three-in-one God is God. Each One has a certain work and each works together with the Others. What Christ was like before the world was made is best seen in John 17:5, "Now, Father, honor Me with the honor I had with You before the world was made." And in John 17:24, "Father, I want My followers You gave Me to be with Me where I am. Then they may see My shining greatness which You gave Me because You loved Me before the world was made." Man does not know what that shining greatness was. When Christ left all the greatness and honor of heaven to come to the earth to live as a man among sinful men, He did not put His greatness aside. He and the Father were One even when He became as one who is owned by someone. (John 14:7-11) Philippians 2:6-7 says, "Jesus has always been as God is. But He did not hold to His rights as God. He put aside everything that belonged to Him and made Himself the same as a servant who is owned by someone. He became human by being born as a man."

CHRIST WAS BORN AS A MAN

The Holy Writings teach that Jehovah of the Old Testament became flesh in the person of Jesus Who was born in the town of Bethlehem. (Matthew 1:18-25; Luke 1:26-35; John 1:14; Acts 10:38; Romans 8:34; Galatians 4:4; I Timothy 3:16; Hebrews 2:14)

The way Christ of heaven became flesh on earth is told in Luke 1:34-35. This does not mean that men can understand how it happened. Ephesians 3:19 says such things go beyond what can be understood. Romans 11:33b says, "No one can understand His thoughts. No one can understand His ways."

Why Christ left heaven to come to earth in human flesh:

1. *TO MAKE THE FATHER KNOWN.* John 1:18, "The much-loved Son is beside the Father. No man has ever seen God. But Christ has made God known to us."

2. *TO UNDERSTAND MAN.* Hebrews 2:18, "Because Jesus was tempted as we are and suffered as we do, He understands us and He is able to help us when we are tempted."

3. *TO TAKE AWAY SINS.* I JOHN 3:5, "You know that Christ came to take away our sins. There is no sin in Him."

4. *TO SHOW MAN HOW TO LIVE.* I Peter 2:21, "These things are all a part of the Christian life to which you have been called. Christ suffered for us. This shows us we are to follow in His steps."

5. *TO DESTROY THE WORKS OF THE DEVIL.* I John 3:8, "The person who keeps on sinning belongs to the devil. The devil has sinned from the beginning. But the Son of God came to destroy the works of the devil."

6. *TO WIN OVER DEATH.* Hebrews 2:14, "It is true that we share the same Father with Jesus. And it is true that we share the same kind of flesh and blood because Jesus became a man like us. He died as we must die. Through His death He destroyed the power of the devil who has the power of death."

7. *TO GET THINGS READY FOR HIS SECOND COMING.* Hebrews 9:28, "It is the same with Christ. He gave Himself once to take away the sins of many. When He comes the second time, He

will not need to give Himself again for sin. He will save all those who are waiting for Him."

Christ came into this world the same as all other men BUT WITHOUT SIN. Because He was without sin, He was able to give Himself for man's sin. Without sin, He was able to take the punishment for man's sins and set man free.

1. CHRIST WAS TRUE MAN.

A. He was born of a women and grew as other men. He looked like a man and got tired like other men. John 4:6 says, "Jacob's well was there. Jesus was tired from traveling so He sat down just as He was by the well. It was about noon."

B. He became hungry. Matthew 4:2 says, "Jesus went without food for forty days and forty nights. After that He was hungry."

C. He became thirsty. John 19:28 says, "Jesus knew that everything was now finished. Everything happened as the Holy Writings said it would happen. He said, 'I am thirsty.' "

D. He chose to call Himself the Son of Man. Matthew 26:64 says, "Jesus said to him, 'What you said is true. I say to you, from now on you will see the Son of Man seated on the right hand of the All-powerful God. You will see Him coming on the clouds of the sky.' "

2. CHRIST WAS ALSO TRUE GOD.

A. He wanted people to worship Him. Matthew 14:33 says, "Those in the boat worshiped Jesus. They said, 'For sure, You are the Son of God!' " Luke 24:52 says, "...they worshiped Him. Then they went back to Jerusalem with great joy." John 20:28 says, "Thomas said to Him, 'My Lord and my God!' " (Isaiah 40:3)

B. He is All-powerful. Matthew 28:18 says, "Jesus came and said to them, 'All power has been given to Me in heaven and on earth.' "

C. He knows all things. John 16:30 says, "Now we are sure You know everything. You do not need anyone to tell You anything. Because of this we believe that You came from God."

D. He is everywhere by the Holy Spirit. Matthew 18:20 says, "For where two or three are gathered together in My name, there I am with them." Matthew 28:20 says, "Teach them to do all things I have told you. And I am with you always, even to the end of the world."

E. When Christ was on trial, He told the leaders that He was God. Matthew 26:63-66 says, "Jesus said nothing. Then the head religious leader said to Him, 'In the name of the living God, I tell You to say the truth. Tell us if You are the Christ, the Son of God.' Jesus said to him, 'What you said is true. I say to you from now on you will see the Son of Man seated on the right hand of the All-powerful God. You will see Him coming on the clouds of the sky.' Then the head religious leader tore his clothes apart. He said, 'He has spoken as if He were God! Do we need other people to speak against Him yet? You have heard Him speak as if He were God! What do you think?' They said, 'He is guilty of death!' "

3. CHRIST WAS THE GOD-MAN.

He is true God and He is true Man. When He became human flesh, He not only became a human person, He also became a part of the whole human family. Yet, He was still one of the Three-in-one God at the same time.

A. Christ is the Religious Leader Who made the way for man to go to God. Hebrews 7:23-28 says, "There had to be many religious leaders during the time of the Old Way of Worship. They died and others had to keep on in their work. But Jesus lives forever. He is the Religious Leader forever. It will never change. And so Jesus is able, now and forever, to save from the punishment of sin all who come to God through Him because He lives forever to pray for them. We need such a Religious Leader Who made the way for man to go to God. Jesus is holy and has no guilt. He has never sinned and is different from sinful men. He has the place of honor above the heavens. Christ is not like other religious leaders. They had to give gifts every day on the altar in worship for their own sins first and then for the sins of the people. Christ did not have to do that. He gave one gift on the altar and that gift was Himself. It was done once and it was for all time. The Law makes religious leaders of men. These men are not perfect. After the Law was given, God spoke with a promise. He made His Son a perfect Religious Leader forever."

B. Christ is going to return to earth again. Acts 1:11 says, "They said, 'You men of the country of Galilee, why do you stand looking up into heaven? This same Jesus Who was taken from you into heaven will return in the same way you saw Him go up into heaven.' " (See Part 9)

CHRIST IS TRUE GOD AND TRUE MAN

It is important to understand that Jesus Christ was both God and man at the same time. He is called the God-Man. It must be remembered that He was perfect God and perfect man in one person. He put aside everything that belonged to Him and He became human by being born as a man, but in no way did He stop being God. (Philippians 2:6-7; Colossians 2:9)

1. IT IS TRUE THAT JESUS WAS GOD.

We read in John 1:1, "The Word (Christ) was in the beginning. The Word was with God. The Word was God." Here the Bible calls Jesus, God. Also in Hebrews 1:8 it says, "But about His Son, He says, 'O God, Your place of power will last forever. Whatever You say in Your nation is right and good.' " (Genesis 1:26)

Christ, as God, is called God, the Son of God, Lord, King of Kings and Lord of Lords. He has all power, knows all, is everywhere, and does not change. He makes things, keeps things going, forgives sins, gives life to the dead, and says who is guilty. He is honored by angels and men and one day all men will bow down before Him and say He is Lord.

Jesus left heaven and came to earth. Through the powerful work of God, Jesus was born in human flesh. This is called the *virgin birth* and it means that the baby to be born came to be inside the mother without a father like other children have. How was Jesus born? "The birth of Jesus Christ was like this: Mary His mother had been promised in marriage to Joseph. Before they were married, it was learned that she was to have a baby by the Holy Spirit" (Matthew 1:18). In Isaiah 7:14, long before Jesus was born, it says, "So the Lord Himself will give you a special thing to see: A young women, who had never had a man will give birth to a son. She will give Him the name Immanuel." Matthew 1:20-23 says, "While he was thinking about this, an angel of the Lord came to him in a dream. The angel said, 'Joseph, son of David, do not be afraid to take Mary as your wife. She is to become a mother by the Holy Spirit. A Son will be born to her. You will give Him the name of Jesus because He will save His people from the punishment of their sins.' This happened as the Lord said it would happen through the early preacher. He said, 'The young woman, who has never had a man, will give birth to a Son. They will give Him the name Immanuel. This means God with us' " (Isaiah 7:14). When Jesus was born, He was born like any baby is born. (Luke 2:6-7) But how He came to be inside Mary was a special powerful work of God by the Holy Spirit.

What was Mary, the Mother of Jesus, like? In Luke 1:26-38 we read of an angel telling Mary that God had chosen her from among many women to be the mother of Jesus by the Holy Spirit. She was chosen because of her faith in God. Mary was a woman of honor to be the mother of Jesus, but she was not without sin. Jesus was born without sin because the Holy Spirit was the One Who made Jesus come to be inside Mary. Jesus showed no special favor to His mother. When His mother and brothers came to see Jesus, He acted as if He did not know they were His own family. (Mark 3:31-35) He said, "Whoever does what My Father wants is My brother and My sister and My mother." The Bible tells us that Mary had other children, brothers and sisters of Jesus. Mark 6:3 says, "Is He not a Man Who makes things from wood? Is He not the Son of Mary and the brother of James and Joses and Judas and Simon? Do not His sisters live here with us?"

2. *IT IS TRUE THAT JESUS WAS MAN.*

The Bible proves to us that Jesus was human in every way.

A. He was born of a woman. (Galatians 4:4)
B. He grew as other people. (Luke 2:52)
C. He became hungry. (Matthew 4:2)
D. He became tired. (John 4:6)
E. He cried. (John 11:35)
F. He died. (Matthew 27:50)

In Philippians 2:6-7 it says, "Jesus has always been as God is. But He did not hold to His rights as God. He put aside everything that belonged to Him and made Himself the same as a servant who is owned by someone. He became human by being born as a man." He did this so He might show man God as well as teach man how to live. He also came to save man from the punishment of sin and to destroy the works of the devil. Because He came, He understands man and makes the way for him to go to God. He proved that God told the truth long ago when He promised that Christ would come.

Jesus Christ was human, a man just like men are today, but it must be understood that He never sinned. He was tempted like man is, but He did not sin. (Hebrews 4:15)

3. *IT IS IMPORTANT TO UNDERSTAND THAT JESUS IS THE TRUE GOD-MAN.*

There are false teachers who say that He did not come in a human body. (I John 4:2-3; 5:20-21) It is hard to understand how Christ was God and man at the same time. But in His life here on earth He was seen as both.

CHRIST THE GOD-MAN

As a man He was tired, and yet as God He called the tired to Himself for rest.

As a man He was hungry, and yet as God He was "The Bread of Life."

As a man He was thirsty, and yet as God He was "The Water of Life."

As a man He was in pain, and yet as God He healed those who were sick and in pain.

As a man He grew, and yet as God He was from the beginning.

As a man He was tempted, and yet as God He could not be tempted.

As a man He did not know everything, and yet as God He knew all things.

As a man He made Himself less important than the angels, and yet as God He was more important than they were.

As a man He said, "My Father is greater than I," and yet as God He said, "I and My Father are one."

As a man He prayed, and yet as God He answered prayer.

As a man He cried at the grave, and yet as God He called the dead to arise.

As a man He died, and yet as God He is life that lasts forever.

CHRIST'S NAMES

There are over 100 names given to Christ in God's Word. These names give Him honor and put Him high above everything. He is the *Holy One, Lord of All,* the *Beginning and the End.* He is *God's only Son,* the *Bright and Morning Star,* and *God's Greatest Gift.* He is called *Wonderful, One Who comes along side to help, The Father that lasts forever,* the *Prince of Peace.* He is also the *King of the Jews,* the *King of Kings,* the *Lord Strong and Powerful,* the *True God,* and *Lord powerful to save.*

1. *THE NAMES AND MEANINGS:*

A. Jesus - This name means *to save, to help, to make free.* Matthew 1:21b says, "...You will give Him the name of Jesus because He will save His people from the punishment of their sins."

B. Christ - The name *Christ* means *One Who was chosen to do a special job* or *Anointed One.* It is the same as *Messiah* in the Old Testament. *Anointing* means to pour oil on a person. In Old Testament times, men chosen for a special job had oil poured over them. At first He was called *Jesus the Christ* but later this was changed to *Jesus Christ.* Matthew 16:16 says, "Simon Peter said, 'You are the Christ, the Son of the living God.' "

C. Lord - Lord means that He is leader of the Church. John 9:38 says, "He said, 'I do put my trust in You, Lord.' Then he got down in front of Jesus and worshiped Him."

D. Son of Man - This was a name Jesus called Himself. It means He was God, and yet He became man. Luke 19:10 says, "For the Son of Man came to look for and to save from the punishment of sin those who are lost."

E. Son of David - This name means that God was telling the truth long ago when He promised Christ would come. Matthew 9:27 says, "Jesus went on from there. Two blind men followed Him. They called out, 'Take pity on us, Son of David.' " (Jeremiah 23:5)

F. Immanuel - This was the name given Christ when He was born. It means *God with us.* Matthew 1:23b says, "...They will give Him the name Immanuel. This means God with us." (Isaiah 7:14)

2. HE IS ALSO CALLED:

A. The Word - which means One Who helps men understand.

B. Teacher - As teacher He taught others.

C. Religious Leader (High Priest) - He goes to God for man. Because of Adam all men were born in sin, but Christ made the way for men's sins to be forgiven.

D. Lamb of God - He was perfect and the only one who could take away sins.

3. MANY NAMES TELL OF THE WORK CHRIST DID:

The *One Who cares for others,* the *One Who saves,* the *Head Shepherd,* and the *One Who helps us out of trouble or danger.*

He is *Faithful, True, Friend of Sinners, Gift of God,* the *Light of the World,* and the *One Who says what is right or wrong.*

He can be trusted because He is the *Rock* and *Corner Stone,* the *Way* and the *Door* to heaven. He is *Life.*

CHRIST'S DEATH

The Old Testament told about the death of Christ. In Genesis 3:15 it says that Satan, the snake, would hurt the Special Person to come. Isaiah 53 tells about Christ putting men's sins on Himself. It shows that the Special Person to come would die. Zechariah 13:6-7 says that the Shepherd would die and the sheep would run away. In John 10 Jesus says that He is that Good Shepherd.

The Old Testament showed in different ways how Christ would die. When Adam and Eve were put out of the garden of Eden, God made coats of skin for them which showed that blood had to be given to make a covering. Adam's son Abel killed a lamb as a gift on the altar in worship. This was a picture of how Christ would die for men. This same picture was shown in Exodus 12 where a lamb was killed and the blood put on the door in a special way to show that sins were covered. In Numbers 21, when Moses made a snake from brass and put it up on a pole for the Jews to see, it showed how Christ would be put up on a cross. Christ talked about that in John 3:14-15.

The New Testament teaches that when Christ died, He died in the place of those who had sinned. I Peter 3:18 teaches that Christ never sinned but God put men's sin on Him so men could be made right with God. II Corinthians 5:21 teaches that Christ let Himself be hated and punished instead of man. Galatians 3:13 teaches that Christ died. Christ had to die as man dies if He was to die in man's place for sin. And yet His death was planned before God made the world and man. Even though He died, His death was different. Matthew 27:50 says, "Jesus...gave up His Spirit and died." He wanted to die for men and He was free to do so. When the soldiers came to kill the men on the crosses, they did not break Jesus' legs as they did the other two who were hanging beside Him. They saw He was already dead, but they cut His side to be sure. When blood and water came out, they were sure He was already dead.

Christ died to give His life for men. He did not die because the court said He must be killed. The nails did not hold Jesus on the cross. He gave His life for others that they might have life. Hebrews 10:10-14 says that He gave Himself as a gift to God. Romans 5:6-9 says that He gave His life for all sinners and that His blood paid the punishment for sin. I John 2:2 says that He paid for the sins of the whole world.

Because Jesus died, men can be saved. (Romans 5:9) Men can be saved or set free from the power of sin over them. (John 8:32-36; Romans 6:10) Men can be saved from being guilty of sin. (Romans 5:16-17) He saved men from the fear of sin. (II Timothy 1:7) Christ saved men through love. (John 4:9-10) So His death paid for the punishment of the sins of all men from Adam to the end of the world.

AS MOSES LIFTED UP THE SNAKE IN THE DESERT, SO THE SON OF MAN MUST BE LIFTED UP.

CHRIST WAS RAISED FROM THE DEAD

The truth that Jesus was raised from the dead after He died on the cross to take the punishment for man's sins is one of the most important truths in the Word of God. Being made right with God depends on this. I Corinthians 15:17 says, "If Christ was not raised from the dead, your faith is worth nothing and you are still living in your sins." A person must believe that Christ was raised from the dead. It has been known for almost two thousand years that Jesus was raised from the dead.

1. *THE TRUTH THAT JESUS WAS RAISED FROM THE DEAD SHOWS MANY THINGS:*

A. It shows that the Lord Jesus finished His work by dying in man's place taking the punishment for his sin. God received Jesus' death in our place.

B. It proves and promises to man that some day Christ will come again. Christ's death on the cross to take the punishment for man's sins would be of no use unless He had been raised from the dead. (Romans 4:25; I Corinthians 15:14,17) We know that God received Christ's finished work, because God raised Christ and put Him in a place of power at God's own right side. (Philippians 2:8-10; Hebrews 1:3) If Christ had not been raised from the dead, He could not have gone to Heaven. And if He had not gone to heaven, He could not come again to take man to heaven with Him. (I Thessalonians 4:14-16; Acts 1:3,9-11) But He was raised from the dead!

C. The truth that Christ was raised from the dead is the greatest truth of all times. (Acts 1:3)

It is the greatest proof of the Christian way of worship. (Romans 1:4)

It is the greatest show of God's power. (Ephesians 1:19-20)

It is the greatest truth of the Good News. (I Corinthians 15:3-4; Romans 10:9-10)

It is the greatest thing to make man believe and trust. (I Thessalonians 4:14)

It is the greatest thing to make sure of man's coming pay for trusting in Christ. (I Corinthians 15:20)

It is the greatest thing to make man want to be holy. (Romans 6:9-12)

D. The truth that Jesus was raised from the dead was so proven to the followers of Christ that they did not have any doubt about it. They went out and preached it without being afraid. They preached this even to people who hated them. They were ready to be killed for preaching it. They told those who were listening that they were guilty of killing Jesus, the very One Whom God raised from the dead. (Acts 2:23-24, 36b; 3:13-15) Those people were very angry but they could not say that those things were not true.

E. After His suffering and death, Jesus showed Himself alive to many of His followers. He was seen by them during the 40 days He was on earth after He was raised from the dead. This is proof that He was raised from the dead.

He showed Himself to many people:

(1) To 500 people who saw Him at one time (I Corinthians 15:6)

(2) To Mary Magdalene (John 20:14-16)

(3) To the women returning from the tomb (Matthew 28:8-10)

(4) To Peter (Luke 24:34)

(5) To His followers toward evening (Luke 24:33-36)

(6) To the two followers on the road to Emmaus (Luke 24:13-31)

(7) To all the missionaries eight days later (John 20:26)

(8) To seven by the lake of Tiberias (John 21:1-23)

(9) To James (I Corinthians 15:7)

(10) To the eleven (Matthew 28:16-20)

(11) To Stephen outside Jerusalem (Acts 7:55)

(12) To Paul near the city of Damascus (Acts 9:3-6)

(13) In the House of God (Acts 22:17-21)

(14) To John on the Island of Patmos (Revelation 1:10-19)

2. *THESE PROVE JESUS WAS RAISED FROM THE DEAD:*

A. The empty grave (Mark 16:5-6)

B. The grave clothes had not been moved. (Luke 24:12)

C. The way Christ acted after being raised from the dead. (Luke 24:36-40)

D. The early church taught it. (Acts 13:29-31)

E. The changed lives of the followers of Christ. (Acts 13:47)

F. The change from sinner to Christian in Saul's life. (Acts 9:1-18)

G. The New Testament proves it.

H. The way Christ gives new life to a person proves this more than anything else.

3. *THE TRUTH THAT JESUS WAS RAISED FROM THE DEAD WAS TALKED ABOUT.*

A. Years ago God showed His people what would happen in the future.

(1) The Old Testament tells about it. (Job 19:25-26; Psalm 16:10)

(2) Christ Himself tells about it. (Matthew 17:22-23; 20:17-19)

(3) God completed what He promised in the Holy Writings. Acts 13:32-33a says, "We bring you the Good News about the promise made to our early fathers. God has finished this for us who are their children. He did this by raising Jesus from the dead." Psalm 2:7b says, "You are My Son. Today I have become Your Father." (Luke 24:45-46)

B. Angels and those who hated Him talked about it. Matthew 28:5-6 says, "The angel said to the women, 'Do not be afraid. I know you are looking for Jesus Who was nailed to the cross. He is not here! He has risen from the dead as He said He would. Come and see the place where the Lord lay.' " (Matthew 28:11-15; Luke 24:1-4,7,23)

4. *SOME OF THE THINGS THAT ARE SHOWN BY CHRIST BEING RAISED FROM THE DEAD:*

A. It shows that God the Father was happy to receive Jesus.

B. It shows that Jesus is God's Only (Unique) Son.

C. It shows how Jesus has won over the devil and death.

D. It shows how Jesus can never be destroyed.

E. It shows how the one who has put his trust in Christ is as if he had never sinned.

F. It shows the power of Christ in the Christian.

G. It gives a living hope to the Christian.

H. It gives the Christian a Religious Leader.

I. It promises the Christian that some day he, too, will be raised from the dead to be with God in Heaven.

J. It shows the world His truth.

K. It tells the world that all men will be raised up some day. They will be told they are guilty and will be punished, or they will receive their pay for living for Christ.

L. It tells the world that someday it will be told it is guilty.

All other religions worship a dead god. Christians are the only people who worship a God Who has won over death and lives today.

CHRIST WAS TAKEN UP TO HEAVEN

1. *THE TRUTH THAT CHRIST HAS BEEN TAKEN UP INTO HEAVEN AND IS AT THE RIGHT SIDE OF THE FATHER AND HAS BEEN GIVEN POWER AND HONOR AND GREATNESS MEANS THAT GOD IS PLEASED WITH THE WORK CHRIST DID TO TAKE AWAY OUR SIN.* (Hebrews 9)

2. *CHRIST'S GOING TO HEAVEN WAS NEEDED.* The giving of power and honor and greatness to Christ was needed:

   A. To finish His work to make men free. (John 20:16-17)

   B. So His followers could do greater works. John 14:12 says, "For sure, I tell you, whoever puts his trust in Me can do the things I am doing. He will do even greater things than these because I am going to the Father."

   C. So the Holy Spirit could be given. John 7:39 says, "Jesus said this about the Holy Spirit Who would come to those who put their trust in Him. The Holy Spirit had not yet been given. Jesus had not yet been raised to the place of honor." (John 16:7)

   D. So what He did could be known over all the world. People over all the world could worship Him. Matthew 28:18-20 says, "Jesus came and said to them, 'All power has been given to Me in heaven and on earth. Go and make followers of all the nations. Baptize them in the name of the Father and of the Son and of the Holy Spirit. Teach them to do all the things I have told you. And I am with you always, even to the end of the world.' "

   E. So His followers, both then and now, would be able to tell others what happened to Jesus after He had died and had been raised from the dead. They saw Him taken up into heaven. Luke 24:50-51 says, "Jesus led them out as far as Bethany. Then He lifted up His hands and prayed that good would come to them. And while He was praying that good would come to them, He went from them and was taken up to heaven and they worshiped Him." (Mark 16:9; Acts 1:9)

3. *CHRIST'S WORK NOW IS PRAYING FOR MEN AS HE SITS AT THE RIGHT SIDE OF GOD IN HEAVEN.* Hebrews 10:12b says, "...He sat down at the right side of God." And Hebrews 7:25 says, "And so Jesus is able, now and forever, to save from the

punishment of sin all who come to God through Him because He lives forever to pray for them." (Isaiah 53:12b; Romans 8:26)

4. *THE TRUTH OF CHRIST BEING TAKEN UP INTO HEAVEN WAS TAUGHT BY:*

A. Peter - Acts 2:32-33 says, "Jesus is this One! God has raised Him up and we have all seen Him. This Jesus has been lifted up to God's right side. The Holy Spirit was promised by the Father. God has given Him to us. That is what you are seeing and hearing now!"

B. Paul - Hebrews 8:1 says, "Now the important thing is this: We have such a Religious Leader Who has made the way for man to go to God. He is the One Who sits at the right side of the All-powerful God in the heavens." (Ephesians 1:20-21; 4:8-10)

C. Stephen - who saw Jesus at God's right side. Acts 7:56 says, "He said, 'See! I see heaven open and the Son of Man standing at the right side of God!' "

D. The Revelation of Jesus Christ as given to John.

CHRIST RECEIVED GREAT HONOR AND A VERY IMPORTANT PLACE

1. *GOD'S WORD TELLS OF CHRIST BEING RAISED FROM THE DEAD AND BEING TAKEN UP TO BE WITH THE FATHER.* He also was raised up to receive great honor and was given a very important place.

   A. His followers, standing on the mountain of Olives, saw Him go up. (Luke 24:50-52) From that time on, they knew He had gone to be with the Father. At the prayer meeting as told in Acts 1, His followers did not expect Him to visit them as he had between the time of His being raised from the dead and going to the Father. They knew He was with the Father.

   B. Right after He went to be with the Father, two angels told His followers of His going. Acts 1:10-11 says, "They were still looking up to heaven, watching Him go. All at once two men dressed in white stood beside them. They said, 'You men of the country of Galilee, why do you stand looking up into heaven? This same Jesus Who was taken from you into heaven will return in the same way you saw Him go up into heaven.' "

   C. As Peter preached to the many people the day the Holy Spirit came on the church, he told of Christ being at the right side of God. Acts 2:33 says, "This Jesus has been lifted up to God's right side. The Holy Spirit was promised by the Father. God has given Him to us. That is what you are seeing and hearing now!"

   D. Just before Stephen was killed, he was allowed to look into heaven, and he said, "See! I see heaven open and the Son of Man standing at the right side of God!" (Acts 7:56)

   E. Paul tells of this. Ephesians 1:20-21 says, "It is the same power that raised Christ from the dead. This place was given to Christ. It is much greater than any king or leader can have. No one else can have this place of honor and power. No one in this world or in the world to come can have such honor and power."

2. *WHAT HAPPENED WHEN CHRIST WAS TAKEN UP TO BE WITH THE FATHER.*

   A. Christ returned to the same place of shining greatness He had before He left. John 17:5 says, "Now Father, honor Me with the honor I had with You before the world was made." (Hebrews 1:8-9; Revelation 5:11-12)

B. After Christ was taken back to heaven, the Holy Spirit came down upon the church. Jesus promised this would happen, and it was one reason He returned to the Father. The Holy Spirit was not given until Christ had been raised to the place of honor. John 16:7 says, "I tell you the truth. It is better for you that I go away. If I do not go, the Helper will not come to you. If I go, I will send Him to you."

C. A new and living way has been opened to man which Christ made possible. Hebrews 10:20-21 says, "We now come to God by the new and living way. Christ made this way for us. He opened the curtain, which was His own body. We have a great Religious Leader over the house of God."

D. Because Christ was raised to the place of honor, man has hope for His return. Acts 2:20-21 says, "The sun will turn dark and the moon will turn to blood before the day of the Lord. His coming will be a great and special day. It will be that whoever calls on the name of the Lord will be saved from the punishment of sin."

The first time He came it was to take care of man's sins. The second time He comes He will take all those who have put their trust in Him to be with Himself. Hebrews 9:28 says, "It is the same with Christ. He gave Himself once to take away the sins of many. When He comes the second time, He will not need to give Himself again for sin. He will save all those who are waiting for Him."

It is from this high place of honor in heaven that Christ will come again. Philippians 3:20-21 says, "But we are citizens of heaven. Christ, the One Who saves from the punishment of sin, will be coming down from heaven again. We are waiting for Him to return. He will change these bodies of ours of the earth and make them new. He will make them like His body of shining greatness. He has the power to do this because He can make all things obey Him."

3. *THERE WERE SPECIAL REASONS CHRIST WAS TAKEN UP TO BE WITH THE FATHER.*

A. To give great honor to God. John 17:1 says, "When Jesus had said these things, He looked up to heaven and said, 'Father, the time has come! Honor Your Son so Your Son may honor You.' "

B. To make it possible for men to put their trust in Him. I Timothy 3:16 says, "It is important to know the secret of God-like living, which is: Christ came to earth as a Man. He was pure in His Spirit. He was seen by angels. The nations heard about Him. Men everywhere put their trust in Him. He was taken up into heaven."

C. To give gifts to men. Ephesians 4:8 says, "The Holy Writings say, 'When Christ went up to heaven, He took those who were held with Him. He gave gifts to men.' "

D. To give the gift of the Holy Spirit. John 16:7 says, "I tell you the truth. It is better for you that I go away. If I do not go, the Helper will not come to you. If I go, I will send Him to you."

E. To make an end to the sin problem. Hebrews 1:3 says, "The Son shines with the shining greatness of the Father. The Son is as God is in every way. It is the Son Who holds up the whole world by the power of His Word. The Son gave His own life so we could be clean from all sin. After He had done that, He sat down on the right side of God in heaven."

F. So that men might go with complete trust to the very place of God's loving-favor. Hebrews 4:14-16 says, "We have a great Religious Leader Who has made the way for man to go to God. He is Jesus, the Son of God, Who has gone to heaven to be with God. Let us keep our trust in Jesus Christ. Our Religious Leader understands how weak we are. Christ was tempted in every way we are tempted, but He did not sin. Let us go with complete trust to the very place of God's loving-favor. We will receive His loving-kindness and have His loving-favor to help us whenever we need it."

G. To make the way ready for men to go to God. Hebrews 6:19-20 says, "This hope is a safe anchor for our souls. It will never move. This hope goes into the Holiest Place of All behind the curtain of heaven. Jesus has already gone there. He has become our Religious Leader forever and has made the way for man to go to God. He is like Melchizedek." (Genesis 14:18-20)

H. To save from sin. Hebrews 7:25 says, "And so Jesus is able, now and forever, to save from the punishment of sin all who come to God through Him because He lives forever to pray for them." (Romans 8:34; Hebrews 9:24)

I. To be man's Religious Leader. Hebrews 8:1 says, "Now the important thing is this: We have such a Religious Leader Who has made the way for man to go to God. He is the One Who sits at the right side of the All-powerful God in the heavens."

J. To answer anything anyone says against Christians. Romans 8:33-34 says, "Who can say anything against the people God has chosen? It is God Who says they are right with Himself. Who then can say we are guilty? It was Christ Jesus Who died. He was raised from the dead. He is on the right side of God praying to Him for us."

K. To give comfort to men by their coming near to God and holding on to the hope they have. Hebrews 10:22-23 says, "And so let us come near to God with a true heart full of faith. Our hearts must be made clean from guilty feelings and our bodies washed with pure water. Let us hold on to the hope we say we have and not be changed. We can trust God that He will do what He promised."

L. To make it possible for us to do greater things. John 14:12 says, "For sure, I tell you, whoever puts his trust in Me can do the things I am doing. He will do even greater things than these because I am going to the Father."

M. To give men a place with Christ in the heavens. Ephesians 2:6 says, "God raised us up from death when He raised up Christ Jesus. He has given us a place with Christ in the heavens." (John 14:1-3)

N. To give Jesus a name that is greater than any other name, so that everyone will give honor to God the Father. Philippians 2:8-9 says, "After He became a man, He gave up His important place and obeyed by dying on a cross. Because of this, God lifted Jesus high above everything else. He gave Him a name that is greater than any other name."

O. To fill all the world with Himself. Ephesians 4:10 says, "Christ Who went down into the deep also went up far above the heavens. He did this to fill all the world with Himself."

P. So that Christ may have the power to rule. Matthew 28:18 says, "Jesus came and said to them, 'All power has been given to Me in heaven and on earth.' " (Acts 3:20-21; Hebrews 10:12-13; I Peter 3:22)

Q. So that Christ could take His right place as head of the church. Colossians 1:18 says, "Christ is the head of the church which is His body. He is the beginning of all things. He is the first to be raised from the dead. He is to have first place in everything." (Ephesians 4:15-16; 5:30-32)

R. To clean the heavens where Satan worked against God. In Hebrews 9:23-24 it says that the blood of animals was used to clean the house of God which was a picture of the house of God in heaven. But heaven needed something better than the blood of animals. It had to have the blood of Christ.

CHRIST SPOKE FOR GOD

In Deuteronomy 18:18-19 it says, "I will give them a man who speaks for God like you from among their brothers. I will put My words in his mouth. And he will make known to them all that I tell him. He will speak in My name. And I will punish whoever will not listen to him." Long ago one of the early preachers said that Christ would be One Who spoke for God. (Acts 3:22)

The first and most important meaning of the word *prophet* is *one who brings things to light.* It also means *one who tells what will happen.* In the Old Testament the name meant: *one who sees,* or *one who sees what the eye does not see.* The New Testament meaning is, *one who spoke to the people must speak what God wanted spoken.* The meaning in both the Old and New Testaments show that Christ was One Who spoke for God.

1. *EARLY PREACHERS SPOKE FOR GOD.*

Many think that a prophet is one who tells only what is going to happen in the future. This is not true. The One who spoke for God during the time of Israel was interested in what *was happening* as well as what *was going to happen* in the future. Much of what those who spoke for God said to the people was about what was happening then. But they also said many things that had to do with the future. God used special men He chose in Old Testament times to speak to His people, but He used Christ to speak to His people in the times of the New Testament. Hebrews 1:1-2a says, "Long ago God spoke to our early fathers in many different ways. He spoke through the early preachers. But in these last days He has spoken to us through His Son."

2. *CHRIST SPOKE FOR GOD.*

Christ was One Who spoke for God from the time He was baptized at the Jordan River until He was nailed to the cross on Calvary. Acts 2:22 says, "Jewish men, listen to what I have to say! You knew Jesus of the town of Nazareth by the powerful works He did. God worked through Jesus while He was with you. You all know this." (Matthew 4:23-25; Luke 4:14-17; Hebrews 9:26-28)

During the time He was on earth, Christ spoke for God about important things in the future:

A. He spoke of His death and about His being raised from the dead. (Matthew 12:39-40; 26:1-2; John 2:19-22)

B. He told what would happen between the time of His death and the time Jerusalem would be destroyed. (Matthew 24:4-14; Mark 13:13; Luke 21:5-24)

C. He told that Jerusalem would be destroyed, and that the Christians would suffer and be killed and be sent everywhere. Also He told about a very sinful man-made god that would stand in the house of God in Jerusalem. (Matthew 24:15-22; Mark 13:14-23; Luke 21:20-28)

D. He told that the Good News would be preached over all the earth. (Matthew 24:14)

E. He told how He would come again to earth. (See Part 9)

3. *IN THE PAST THERE HAVE BEEN "FALSE PREACHERS," AND THERE ARE MANY TODAY. CERTAIN TESTS SHOW IF THEY ARE "FALSE PREACHERS."*

A. Christ gave a test that can be used today. "So you will know them by their fruit" (Matthew 7:20). They try to prove they are ones who speak for God by doing powerful things, but they are false.

B. If early preachers did not preach against sin and tell men to be sorry for their sin and turn from it, they were false. It is the same today.

C. False preachers can be tested by the Word of God. Even if they do all kinds of things that look like powerful works, if what they say is not true to what the Word of God says, they are false.

D. The spirits can be tested. I John 4:13 says, "Dear Christian friends, do not believe every spirit. But test the spirits to see if they are from God for there are many false preachers in the world. You can tell if the spirit is from God in this way: Every spirit that says Jesus Christ has come in a human body is from God. And every spirit that does not say Jesus has come in a human body is not from God. It is the teaching of the false-christ. You have heard that this teaching is coming. It is already here in the world."

CHRIST IS MAN'S RELIGIOUS LEADER WHO HAS MADE THE WAY FOR HIM TO GO TO GOD

A religious leader is one who stands between God and man, and prays to the perfect God for the guilty sinner. The Word of God tells that Christ is our Religious Leader. Hebrews 5:6; 6:20 say, "God says in another part of His Word, 'You will be a Religious Leader forever. You will be like Melchizedek.' " "Jesus has already gone there. He has become our Religious Leader forever and has made the way for man to go to God. He is like Melchizedek." (Psalm 110:4)

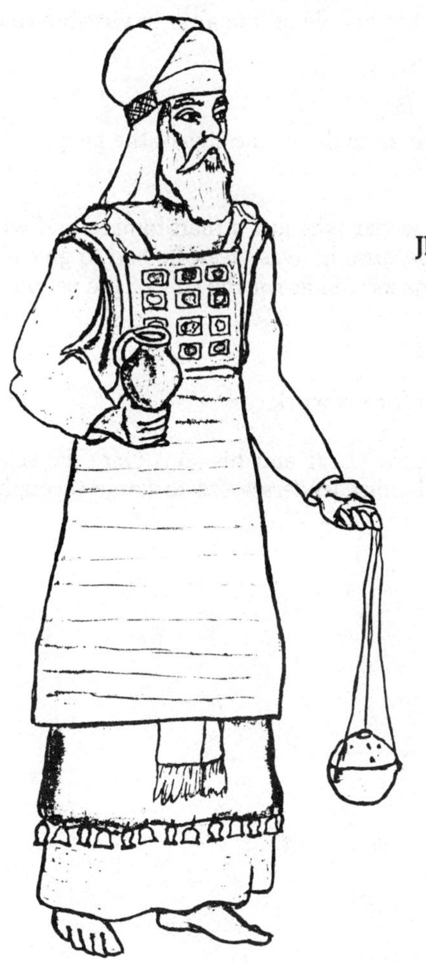

THIS IS HOW THE JEWISH HIGH PRIEST DRESSED

1. CHRIST WAS ALL THE THINGS A RELIGIOUS LEADER HAD TO BE.

A. In the Old Way of Worship there were special religious leaders for the Jewish people. These men were called *priests* and they were helpers standing between God and man. In Hebrews 5:1-4 it tells what a religious leader had to be:

(1) He was chosen from among men. →

(2) He was a helper standing between God and man. →

(3) He gave gifts from the people on the altar in worship to God. →

(4) He gave blood from animals for the sins of the people. →

(5) A Jewish religious leader was just a man himself and weak in many ways. And because he was weak he had to give gifts to God for his own sins as well as for the sins of the people. →

(6) God chose the man for his work. →

(7) Under the Jewish Law, Levi and his sons were the religious leaders, and all religious leaders were to come through that family. (Hebrews 7:11) →

B. Jesus Christ is man's Religious Leader Who has made the way for man to go to God. Christ could be man's Religious Leader because:

→ (1) He was chosen from among men. (Hebrews 5:4-6)

→ (2) He was more than a helper standing between God and men. He is man's Religious Leader Who made the way for him to go to God.

→ (3) Christ gave only one gift on the altar and that was Himself. He was a perfect gift and never again does a gift have to be given for man's sins. (Hebrews 9:25-26)

→ (4) Christ gave His own blood, not the blood of animals like the other religious leaders did.

→ (5) Jesus Christ, man's Religious Leader, is holy and has no guilt. He has never sinned and is different from sinful men. (Hebrews 7:26) That is why He could give Himself as a gift for all men and not have to give one for Himself like the other religious leaders did.

→ (6) God chose Christ to be man's Religious Leader. (Hebrews 5:6)

→ (7) Jesus did not come from the family of Levi but from the family of Judah. Those from the family of Levi were not able to give gifts which would last forever on the altar for the sins of the people. God changed this. Jesus was from another family, and He was the Gift which was perfect in every way. He then could be given for the sins of the people. (Hebrews 7:11-14)

2. *CHRIST DID ALL THE THINGS A RELIGIOUS LEADER HAD TO DO.*

A. In the Old Way of Worship the religious leader did three special things:

(1) He killed animals and gave them on the altar as a gift in worship for the people. →

(2) He went inside the Holy Place to pray for the people. The head religious leader went into the Holiest Place of All once a year taking the blood of an animal to give for his own sins and for the sins of all the people. (Hebrews 9:6-7) →

(3) After he gave the blood in the Holiest Place of All, he came out. Then he gave thanks and prayed that good would come to the people. →

B. As our great Religious Leader, Christ did all three things:

→ (1) He gave Himself as a gift on the altar. Hebrews 9:14 says, "How much more the blood of Christ will do! He gave Himself as a perfect gift to God through the Spirit that lives forever. Now your heart can be free from the guilty feeling of doing work that is worth nothing. Now you can work for the living God."

→ (2) Christ is now praying to God for man. Romans 8:34 says, "Who then can say we are guilty? It was Christ Jesus Who died. He was raised from the dead. He is on the right side of God praying to Him for us." Hebrews 7:25 says, "And so Jesus is able, now and forever, to save from the punishment of sin all who come to God through Him because He lives forever to pray for them."

→ (3) When Christ comes to earth the second time, He will take with Him all those who have put their trust in Him. Hebrews 9:28 says, "It is the same with Christ. He gave Himself once to take away the sins of many. When He comes the second time He will not need to give Himself again for sin. He will save all those who are waiting for Him." (I Thessalonians 4:16; I Peter 1:5; Revelation 20:4)

Hebrews 4:15-16 says, "Our Religious Leader understands how weak we are. Christ was tempted in every way we are tempted, but He did not sin. Let us go with complete trust to the very place of God's loving-favor. We will receive His loving-kindness and have His loving-favor to help us whenever we need it."

CHRIST'S DEATH IN MAN'S PLACE

The word *atonement* means the work of Christ when He gave Himself to pay for the sins of guilty sinners to satisfy God Who, being holy, hates sin. This was done by Christ's holy life, His death on the cross in place of the sinner, His being raised from the dead, and His receiving great honor in heaven.

The word *atonement* is not found in most translations of the Bible, but it is often used when speaking about the work of Christ. God gave what was needed to make peace between the sinner and Himself. Man did not make a way, God took care of it for man. Man could never work his way up to God. God came down to man to take care of his need.

1. THE TEACHING OF CHRIST'S DEATH IN OUR PLACE IS IMPORTANT BOTH IN HEAVEN AND ON EARTH.

A. It is one of the things the angels wanted to know about. I Peter 1:11-12 says, "The early preachers wondered at what time or to what person this would happen. The Spirit of Christ in them was talking to them and told them to write about how Christ would suffer and about His shining greatness later on. They knew these would not happen during the time they lived but while you are living many years later. These are the very things that were told to you by those who preached the Good News. The Holy Spirit Who was sent from heaven gave them power and they told of things that even the angels would like to know about."

B. Christ Himself said this was the most important part of His work. Mark 10:45 says, "For the Son of Man did not come to be cared for. He came to care for others. He came to give His life so that many could be bought by His blood and be made free from sin."

C. Christ knew this teaching would attract men to Him. John 12:32 says, "And when I am lifted up from the earth, I will attract all people toward me."

D. The Holy Writings tell much about Christ giving Himself for sinners. The death of Christ is spoken of more than 175 times in the New Testament. Paul speaks of it often, as do other New Testament writers.

God's loving-favor to man means love in action. Even before man knew what his need was, God took care of it. Romans 4:25; 5:6 say, "Jesus died for our sins. He was raised from the dead to make us right with God." "We were weak and could not help ourselves. Then Christ came at the right time and gave His life for all sinners."

There are many religions that tell men they can go to God after they become good. This is not true. God's Word says that He makes men know they are sinners and gives them a desire to be free from sin. False ways of worship try to take men to God. But men, being sinners, are not ready to stand before God. The true way of worship is possible because God became man, and in doing so, He made the way for men to go to Himself.

2. *FOUR REASONS WHY CHRIST HAD TO DIE IN MAN'S PLACE:*

A. God is holy. When man first sinned, this was not pleasing to God. God, being holy, hates sin. But God is not only holy, He is also love. He loved man, not because man had no sin, but while man was a sinner. Romans 5:8 says, "But God showed His love to us. While we were still sinners, Christ died for us."

Even if a sinner stopped doing bad things, it would not change his desires and thoughts. The sinner would still be at war with God. God is holy and He cannot forget these things. He cannot love the sin, but He does love the sinner. The answer to this problem was in the death of Christ, God's own Son. Christ took upon Himself the punishment that should have been given to the sinner. Because God is holy, something had to be done. His Son did something about it. He died in our place.

B. The Laws of God were broken so a gift had to be given to God. Only a perfect gift could be given on the altar in worship. Christ was that Perfect Gift. He is the only One Who could be a gift on the altar for the sinner.

C. When a man sins, his heart tells him that he is guilty. Peace and rest cannot come until the sinner knows that his sin is forgiven. When the sinner knows that Christ took his punishment upon Himself, peace and rest come to him. Romans 5:1 says, "Now that we have been made right with God by putting our trust in Him, we have peace with Him. It is because of what our Lord Jesus Christ did for us."

D. The lost sinner knows he is lost. His heart tells him that he is guilty. When the Holy Spirit speaks to him through the Word of God, he sees how much he has broken God's Law, and how lost he is. If man is to be saved from sin, the One Who never sinned must find him and save him. This is just what Christ did. Luke

19:10 says, "For the Son of Man came to look for and to save from the punishment of sin those who are lost."

3. *WHAT CHRIST DID WHEN HE DIED IN OUR PLACE WAS IMPORTANT BECAUSE:*

A. It was the most important reason for Christ being born. (Matthew 1:21)

B. It has an important place in the first four books of the New Testament. Each of the four writers of these books told many things. But with great care they told about the life and death of Christ. Of the twenty-one chapters in the book of John, ten of them tell of the things leading to Christ's death and of His being raised from the dead.

C. Christ came to earth to show that what God had promised to the early fathers was true. Through the Old Way of Worship, God at different times had promised to send His Son into the world. (Romans 15:8; II Timothy 1:9; II Peter 1:10-12)

D. Christ became a man so He could make His Father known. "No man has ever seen God. But Christ has made God known to us" (John 1:18b). Jesus taught us many things about God the Father. He taught us that God the Father loves us. John 16:27 says, "...because the Father loves you. He loves you because you love Me and believe that I came from the Father."

E. Christ came to be the Religious Leader Who made the way for man to go to God. In the book of Hebrews it teaches us that the head Jewish religious leaders were taken from among men so that they would act in the place of men. (Hebrews 5:1-2) In Hebrews 5:4-5 it also tells us that in the same way, Christ was taken from among men so He could act in the place of men before God.

Hebrews 2:17-18 says, "So Jesus had to become like His brothers in every way. He had to be one of us to be our Religious Leader to go between God and us. He had loving-pity on us and He was faithful. He gave Himself as a gift to die on a cross for our sins so that God would not hold these sins against us any longer. Because Jesus was tempted as we are and suffered as we do, He understands us and He is able to help us when we are tempted."

I Corinthians 10:13 says, "You have never been tempted to sin in any different way than other people. God is faithful. He will not allow you to be tempted more than you can take. But when you are tempted, He will make a way for you to keep from falling into sin."

F. Christ died so that He could destroy sin. "He gave Himself to destroy sin" (Hebrews 9:26b). (Mark 10:45b; John 3-5; II Corinthians 5:21; Romans 5:21; 6:12-18; Hebrews 2:8)

G. Christ died to destroy the works of the devil. "But the Son of God came to destroy the works of the devil" (I John 3:8b). (John 12:31; Hebrews 2:14-15; Revelation 20:10a)

H. Christ died to make ready for the time He will come again. "...when He comes the second time, He will not need to give Himself again for sin" (Hebrews 9:28). (Romans 8:18-25; Revelation 21:27)

I. Christ died so those who have put their trust in Him might have life, "a great full life." (John 10:10b; Romans 5:1; 8:1-3; Hebrews 2:14-15; I John 4:10)

4. *WHO DID CHRIST DIE FOR?*

I Timothy 2:6 says, "He gave His life for all men so they could go free and not be held by the power of sin..." Hebrews 2:9 says, "But we do see Jesus. For a little while He took a place that was not as important as the angels. But God had loving-favor for everyone. He had Jesus suffer death on a cross, for all of us. Then, because of Christ's death on a cross, God gave Him the prize of honor and shining greatness." I John 2:2 says, "He paid for our sins with His own blood. He did not pay for ours only, but for the sins of the whole world."

But the *atonement* is good only for those who take God's Gift. God loves all sinners, but only those who put their trust in Him will be saved from sin. Romans 10:9 says, "If you say with your mouth that Jesus is Lord, and believe in your heart that God raised Him from the dead, you will be saved from the punishment of sin."

Christ divided time. All things before Christ were done looking forward to Christ's birth. All the things that happened after Christ's death look back to what He did when He died on the cross. Christ said, "No one can have greater love than to give his life for his friends" (John 15:13). Men have given their lives for their friends, but Christ had great love for those who were not even His friends.

Romans 5:8 says, "But God showed His love to us. While we were still sinners, Christ died for us." He came from heaven to the cross and bowed His head in a death of shame and pain. His was the greatest gift that was ever given to men. "For God so loved the world that He gave His only Son. Whoever puts his trust in God's Son will not be lost, but will have life that lasts forever" (John 3:16).

THERE IS SOMETHING MAN MUST DO

Man knows he is not right with God. He knows he is a sinner and is lost. There is nothing man can do in his own power to become right with God.

1. *MAN MUST BELIEVE THERE IS A GOD*

   In Hebrews 11:6 it says, "...Anyone who comes to God must believe that He is..." When a man believes, he is sure of a truth and accepts it as truth. It is not only important that he believes God is, but also that he believes Christ died to save sinners, and was raised up from the grave to be the living One Who saves from the punishment of sin. (Isaiah 53:1-12; I Corinthians 15:3-4)

   But believing, alone, is not enough. In James 2:19 it says, "You believe there is one God. That is good! But even the demons believe that, and because they do, they shake." The demons of Satan believe (that is, they know of the truth and accept it as truth) but they do no more than believe.

2. *MAN MUST HAVE FAITH IN GOD.*

   Hebrews 11:6a says, "A man cannot please God unless he has faith." In Hebrews 11:1 it tells what faith is. "Now faith is being sure we will get what we hope for. It is being sure of what we cannot see." If a man only believes that there is a God, but does not have faith in Him, then he is not saved from the punishment of his sin.

3. *MAN MUST TRUST CHRIST TO SAVE HIM FROM HIS SIN.*

   Trust is the action that goes along with believing and faith. Trust is different than believing or faith. This trust means to put one's self into the care of the One in Whom he has faith.

4. *MAN MUST BE SORRY FOR HIS SINS AND TURN FROM THEM.*

   This is called *repentance.* It is a change of one's heart and mind that will lead to a change in what he will do.

   It is possible to feel sorry because of sin, and yet have no desire to stop. The rich man in hell cried out for loving-kindness. He was full of sorrow but it was too late to be sorry for his sins and turn from them.

Luke 16:24-28 says, "He cried out and said, 'Father Abraham, take pity on me. Send Lazarus. Let him put the end of his finger in water and cool my tongue. I am in much pain in this fire.' Abraham said, 'My son, do not forget that when you were living you had your good things. Lazarus had bad things. Now he is well cared for. You are in pain. And more than all this, there is a big deep place between us. No one from here can go there even if he wanted to go. No one can come from there.' Then the rich man said, 'Father, then I beg you to send Lazarus to my father's house. I have five brothers. Let him tell them of these things, or they will come to this place of much pain also.' "

Those who are not sorry for their sins now and will not turn from them will some day cry and grind their teeth. They will have sorrow, but it is not the same as being sorry now.

5. *MAN MUST TELL HIS SINS TO GOD, AND TELL OF GOD TO OTHER MEN.*

A. To God - God wants man to tell his sins to Him so He can forgive him. I John 1:9 says, "If we tell Him our sins, He is faithful and we can depend on Him to forgive our sins. He will make our lives clean from all sin."

B. To men - Men who have put their trust in Christ as the One Who saves must tell other men what has been done in their lives. Romans 10:10b says, "...We tell with our mouth how we were saved from the punishment of sin."

THERE ARE SOME THINGS THAT HAPPEN WHEN A MAN PUTS HIS TRUST IN CHRIST

1. *HE BECOMES A NEW PERSON.*

   II Corinthians 5:17 says, "For if a man belongs to Christ, he is a new person. The old life is gone. New life has begun."

2. *HE IS GIVEN A NEW LIFE.*

   Titus 3:4-5 says, "But God, the One Who saves, showed how kind He was and how He loved us by saving us from the punishment of sin. It was not because we worked to be right with God. It was because of His loving-kindness that He washed our sins away. At the same time He gave us new life when the Holy Spirit came into our lives."

3. *HE IS MADE RIGHT WITH GOD.*

   Romans 3:24 says, "Anyone can be made right with God by the free gift of His loving-favor. It is Jesus Christ Who bought them with His blood and made them free from their sins." (Romans 4:24)

4. *HE IS SAVED FROM THE PUNISHMENT OF SIN, AND ITS GUILT AND BLAME.*

   Romans 5:9 says, "Now that we have been saved from the punishment of sin by the blood of Christ, He will save us from God's anger also." (Ephesians 2:5,8)

5. *HE IS BOUGHT AND MADE FREE FROM SIN.*

   Ephesians 1:7 says, "Because of the blood of Christ, we are bought and made free from the punishment of sin. And because of His blood, our sins are forgiven. His loving-favor to us is so rich." (I Peter 1:19)

6. *HE IS IN GOD'S FAMILY.*

   Ephesians 2:19 says, "From now on you are not strangers and people who are not citizens. You are citizens together with those who belong to God. You belong in God's family." (Romans 8:15, 23; 9:4; II Corinthians 6:17-18; Galatians 3:26; 4:4-7; Ephesians 1:4-11; I John 3:2)

7. *HE IS BAPTIZED INTO THE BODY OF CHRIST BY THE HOLY SPIRIT.*

   I Corinthians 12:13 says, "It is the same way with us. Jews or those who are not Jews, men who are owned by someone or men who are free to do what they want to do, have all been baptized into the one body by the same Holy Spirit. We have all received the one Spirit."

8. *HE IS A PART OF GOD'S BUILDING.*

   Ephesians 2:22 says, "You are also being put together as a part of this building because God lives in you by His Spirit."

9. *HE IS GIVEN A PLACE WITH CHRIST IN HEAVEN.*

   Ephesians 2:6 says, "God raised us up from death when He raised up Christ Jesus. He has given us a place with Christ in the heavens."

10. *HE IS MARKED FOR GOD BY THE HOLY SPIRIT.*

    Ephesians 1:13 says, "The truth is the Good News. When you heard the truth, you put your trust in Christ. Then God marked you by giving you His Holy Spirit as a promise."

11. *HE IS SET APART FOR GOD-LIKE LIVING.*

    I Corinthians 6:11 says, "Some of you were like that. But now your sins are washed away. You were set apart for God-like living to do His work. You were made right with God through our Lord Jesus Christ by the Spirit of our God."

12. *HE RECEIVES GIFTS FROM THE HOLY SPIRIT.*

    I Corinthians 12:4-11 says, "There are different kinds of gifts. But it is the same Holy Spirit Who gives them. There are different kinds of work to be done for Him. But the work is for the same Lord. There are different ways of doing His work. But it is the same God who uses all these ways in all people. The Holy Spirit works in each person in one way or another for the good of all. One person is given the gift of teaching words of wisdom. Another person is given the gift of teaching what he has learned and knows. These gifts are by the same Holy Spirit. One person receives the gift of faith. Another person receives the gifts of healing. These gifts are given by the same Holy Spirit. One person is given the gift of doing powerful works. Another person is given the gift of speaking God's Word. Another person is given the gift of speaking in special sounds. Another person is given the gift of telling what these special sounds mean. But it is the same Holy Spirit, the Spirit of God, Who does all these things. He gives to each person as He wants to give." (Romans 12:5-8; Ephesians 4:11-12)

PART 4

WHAT THE WORD OF GOD TEACHES ABOUT THE HOLY SPIRIT

[*Pneumatology*]

The Person Of The Holy Spirit

The Work Of The Holy Spirit

WHO THE HOLY SPIRIT IS

The Holy Spirit is part of the Three-in-one God.

1. THE HOLY SPIRIT IS GOD.

A. Acts 5:3-4 says, "Peter said to Ananias, 'Why did you let Satan fill your heart? He made you lie to the Holy Spirit...You have lied to God, not to men.' " (I Corinthians 3:16-17)

B. He is as God is.

(1) He has all power. Luke 1:35 says, "The Holy Spirit will come on you. The power of the Most High will cover you." (Romans 15:13-19)

(2) He knows all things. I Corinthians 2:10 says, "It is the Holy Spirit Who Looks into all things, even the secrets of God." (Luke 2:25-32)

(3) He is everywhere. Psalm 139:7-10 says, "Where can I go from Your Spirit? Or where can I run away from where You are? If I go up to heaven, You are there! If I make my bed in the place of the dead, You are there! If I take the wings of the morning or live in the farthest part of the sea, even there Your hand will lead me and Your right hand will hold me."

(4) He is alive forever. Hebrews 9:14b says, "...He gave Himself as a perfect gift to God through the Spirit that lives forever."

This is also shown by Christ when He told His followers to preach the Good News everywhere. He said to baptize in the name of all three of the Three-in-one God. Matthew 28:18-20 says, "Jesus came and said to them, 'All power has been given to Me in heaven and on earth. Go and make followers of all the nations. Baptize them in the name of the Father and of the Son and of the Holy Spirit. Teach them to do all the things I have told you. And I am with you always, even to the end of the world.' "

To end a letter, the missionaries would often write, "May you have loving-favor from our Lord Jesus Christ. May you have the love of God. May you be joined together by the Holy Spirit." The early missionaries spoke of Him as God.

The Revelation of Jesus Christ to John tells of the Holy Spirit as Someone Who should be listened to, "Then listen to what the Spirit says to the churches" Revelation 3:22b).

The work of the church is done by people through gifts given by the Holy Spirit. "There are different kinds of gifts. But it is the same Holy Spirit Who gives them...But it is the same God Who uses all these ways in all people" (I Corinthians 12:4-6). God and the Holy Spirit are spoken of as One in the Bible.

NAMES OF THE HOLY SPIRIT

It is hard for people to understand or learn about someone they cannot touch with their hands or see with their eyes. This is the way with the Holy Spirit. He is part of the Three-in-one God, but He cannot be touched or seen. The Holy Spirit should not be called *It*. The Holy Spirit is a person, and should be called *He* just as God the Father and Christ is a person, and should be called *He*. He has the power to know, the power to feel, and the power to choose. In John 14:16; 16:7 He is called the Helper, or *One called along side to help*. Such a name can be given only to a person. The Holy Spirit took Jesus' place when Jesus left the earth. Such a work as the Holy Spirit does can be done only by a person.

It is important to learn some of the names of the Holy Spirit and then He can be understood better.

1. NAMES OF THE HOLY SPIRIT:

A. The Holy Spirit - Matthew 4:1 says, "Jesus was led by the Holy Spirit to the desert. There He was tempted by the devil."

B. The Spirit of Truth - John 14:17 says, "He is the Spirit of Truth. The world cannot receive Him. It does not see Him or know Him. You know Him because He lives with you and will be in you."

C. The Helper - John 14:26 says, "The Helper is the Holy Spirit. The Father will send Him in My place. He will teach you everything and help you remember everything I have told you."

D. God's Spirit - Romans 8:9 says, "But you are not doing what your sinful old selves want you to do. You are doing what the Holy Spirit tells you to do, if you have God's Spirit living in you. No one belongs to Christ if he does not have Christ's Spirit in him."

E. Christ's Spirit - (Romans 8:9)

F. The Spirit of the Living God - II Corinthians 3:3 says, "You are as a letter from Christ written by us. You are not written as other letters are written with ink on pieces of stone. You are written in human hearts by the Spirit of the Living God."

G. His Holy Spirit of promise - Ephesians 1:13 says, "The truth is the Good News. When you heard the truth, you put your trust in Christ. Then God marked you by giving you His Holy Spirit as a promise."

H. His Spirit - Ephesians 1:17 says, "I pray that the great God and Father of our Lord Jesus Christ may give you the wisdom of His Spirit. Then you will be able to understand the secrets about Him as you know Him better."

I. God's Holy Spirit - Ephesians 4:30 says, "Do not make God's Holy Spirit have sorrow for the way you live. The Holy Spirit has put a mark on you for the day you will be set free.

J. The Spirit that lives forever - Hebrews 9:14 says, "How much more the blood of Christ will do! He gave Himself as a perfect gift to God through the Spirit that lives forever. Now your heart can be free from the guilty feeling of doing work that is worth nothing. Now you can work for the living God."

K. The Spirit - Revelation 2:7, 11, 29 say, "You have ears! Then listen to what the Spirit says to the churches. I will give the fruit of the tree of life in the garden of God to everyone who has power and wins." "You have ears! Then listen to what the Spirit says to the churches. The person who has power and wins will not be hurt by the second death!" "You have ears! Then listen to what the Spirit says to the churches!"

WHAT THE HOLY SPIRIT IS LIKE

Men cannot see the Holy Spirit as they saw Christ when He was on earth. Just as no one has seen God the Father at anytime, no one has seen the Holy Spirit. The Bible gives different pictures that show what the Holy Spirit is like.

1. WHAT THE HOLY SPIRIT IS LIKE:

A. He is like a dove. John 1:32 says, "I saw the Holy Spirit come down on Jesus as a dove from heaven. The Holy Spirit stayed on Him."

B. He is like water. In John 7:38 Jesus says, "The Holy Writings say that rivers of living water will flow from the heart of the one who puts his trust in Me." John 7:39 says, "Jesus said this about the Holy Spirit Who would come to those who put their trust in Him. The Holy Spirit had not yet been given. Jesus had not yet been raised to the place of honor." What water means to thirsty lips or rain to dry ground, the Holy Spirit means to a Christian. Nothing makes thirst end like water and nothing makes the heart as happy as the Holy Spirit.

C. He is like oil. I Samuel 16:13 says, "Then Samuel took the horn of oil and poured the oil on him in front of his brothers. The Spirit of the Lord came upon David with strength from that day on." When people poured oil over someone it was a way to show that God was covering them with Himself. When a person was being set apart to be a religious leader, oil was put first on his ear so he would always hear God's Word. Then oil was put on his thumb so everything he did would bring shining greatness to God. And then oil was put on his toe because he was to walk with God. These things are what the Holy Spirit does in the life of a Christian.

D. He is like wind. John 3:8 says, "The wind blows where it wants to and you hear its sound. You do not know where it comes from or where it goes. It is the same with everyone who is born of the Spirit of God." When the Holy Spirit came down upon the followers after Jesus went to heaven, it says in Acts 2:2, "All at once there was a sound from heaven like a powerful wind. It filled the house where they were sitting." You cannot see wind, yet you can feel it and can see its power. It is this way with the Holy Spirit.

E. He is like fire. Acts 2:3 says, "Then they saw tongues which were divided that looked like fire. These came down on each one of them." After Jesus went to heaven, the Holy Spirit was sent to come on His followers. Tongues of fire were seen above their heads. Fire burns away waste and makes things clean. Burning gives heat. It also gives light to see, and can give power and strength to things being made. All these are pictures of the Holy Spirit. He takes the bad out of men's lives and makes them clean. He makes their hearts hungry for God and gives them a desire to love God. He also tests them to see if they are faithful to God.

F. He is like clothing. Judges 6:34a says, "But the Spirit of the Lord came upon Gideon." The word *came* means *putting on clothes.* He covered Gideon. The Holy Spirit covers His people.

HOW THE HOLY SPIRIT CAN BE HURT

It must be remembered that the Holy Spirit is a person, just as the Son and the Father are persons. With this in mind, it is easier to understand that the Holy Spirit can be hurt. It is because of His loving-kindness that He can be hurt.

1. *HOW THE HOLY SPIRIT CAN BE HURT BY THOSE WHO ARE NOT CHRISTIANS:*

People who have not put their trust in Jesus Christ can hurt the Holy Spirit. He wants to work in their lives so they will put their trust in Jesus Christ. Here are three ways people who are not Christians can hurt the Holy Spirit when He tries to show them the truth about sin.

A. The Holy Spirit can be hurt by those who have hearts that will not listen to Him. Acts 7:51 says, "You have hard hearts and ears that will not listen to me! You are always working against the Holy Spirit. Your early fathers did. You do too." It is sad to see how the Holy Spirit is hurt when He is working in the lives of people to bring them to see their need of putting their trust in Jesus Christ.

B. The Holy Spirit is hurt when He is showing the sinner God's loving-favor, but is laughed at.

C. The Holy Spirit can be hurt if bad words are spoken against Him. The person who does this will not be forgiven. Matthew 12:31-32 says, "I tell you, every sin and every bad word men speak against God will be forgiven, but bad words spoken against the Holy Spirit will not be forgiven. Whoever speaks a word against the Son of Man will be forgiven, but whoever speaks against the Holy Spirit will not be forgiven in this life or in the life to come."

This *could* mean that anyone who says bad words against the special birth of Christ, or says that God's Word is not true, or says that God did not make the world is saying bad words against the Holy Spirit. The Holy Spirit is the One Who gave the words to the men of God who wrote them down. The Holy Spirit is the One Who came upon Mary so that she could give birth to Jesus. The Holy Spirit is the One Who made the world, as it is written in the first chapters of Genesis. To say things against what the Holy Spirit has done is hurting Him. The Bible says that a person who speaks against the Holy Spirit will never be forgiven.

2. *HOW THE HOLY SPIRIT CAN BE HURT BY CHRISTIANS:*

A. The Holy Spirit lives in the Christian to be his Helper. He wants to work in the Christian's life to make him free from his sinful old self. In Galatians 5:16-17 it says, "I say this to you: Let the Holy Spirit lead you in each step. Then you will not please your sinful old selves. The things our old selves want to do are against what the Holy Spirit wants. The Holy Spirit does not agree with what our sinful old selves want. These two are against each other. So you cannot do what you want to do." (Also read verses 19-21 because they tell what the old sinful self is like.)

B. In Ephesians 4:30 it shows how the Christian can hurt the Holy Spirit and cause Him to have sorrow for the way he lives. It says, "Do not make God's Holy Spirit have sorrow for the way you live. The Holy Spirit has put a mark on you for the day you will be set free."

C. The Christian can stop the work of the Holy Spirit in his life if he stops obeying Him. Acts 5:32b says, "...God gives His Spirit to those who obey Him." I Thessalonians 5:19 says, "Do not try to stop the work of the Holy Spirit."

THE HOLY SPIRIT'S WORK BEFORE THE CHURCH BEGAN

1. *THE HOLY SPIRIT, AS PART OF THE THREE-IN-ONE GOD, HAS ALWAYS BEEN AND ALWAYS WILL BE.*

2. *EACH OF THE THREE-IN-ONE GOD HAD A PART OF THE WORK IN MAKING THE WORLD AND IN KEEPING IT GOING.*

   A. The Father - Genesis 1:1 says, "In the beginning God made from nothing the heavens and the earth."

   B. Jesus Christ - Colossians 1:16 says, "Christ made everything in the heavens and on the earth. He made everything that is seen and things that are not seen. He made all the powers of heaven. Everything was made by Him and for Him."

   C. The Holy Spirit - Genesis 1:2b says, "And the Spirit of God was moving over the top of the waters." Job 33:4 says, "The Spirit of God has made me. And the breath of the All-powerful gives me life."

3. *THE WORK OF THE HOLY SPIRIT IS TO KEEP ALL LIVING THINGS GOING AS THEY WERE PLANNED.*

   He brings beauty to the world and keeps everything in its right place. Job 26:13a says, "By His breath the heavens are made beautiful." The Holy Spirit had a part in placing and keeping the heavens in their right place. The work of the Holy Spirit is to give life to man. The Holy Spirit has an important work in the whole world today.

   A. He keeps making the face of the earth new. (Psalm 104:30)

   B. He keeps plant life growing. (Psalm 104:10-13)

   C. He keeps animal and human life growing. (Job 33:4; Psalm 104:11, 12, 14, 21, 27)

4. *THE HOLY SPIRIT DID CERTAIN THINGS DURING THE OLD WAY OF WORSHIP.*

   A. He had a part in telling the early preachers where and what they should preach. (II Peter 1:19-21)

B. He had a part in telling the future. He was the One Who brought the Word of God to the minds of the early preachers who wrote about the future. (I Peter 1:10-12)

5. *THE HOLY SPIRIT GAVE THE HOLY WRITINGS TO MAN.*

(See Part 2, Chapter 11; II Samuel 23:2; Isaiah 1:2; Jeremiah 1:4; Ezekiel 1:3; II Peter 1:20-21)

6. *THE HOLY SPIRIT IS THE ONE WHO TELLS WHAT THE HOLY WRITINGS MEAN.*

In I Corinthians 2:9-14 it says, "The Holy Writings say, 'No eye has ever seen or no ear has ever heard or no mind has ever thought of the wonderful things God has made ready for those who love Him.' God has shown these things to us through His Holy Spirit. It is the Holy Spirit Who looks into all things, even the secrets of God, and shows them to us. Who can know the things about a man, except a man's own spirit that is in him? It is the same with God. Who can understand Him except the Holy Spirit? We have not received the spirit of the world. God has given us His Holy Spirit that we may know about the things given to us by Him. We speak about these things also. We do not use words of man's wisdom. We use words given to us by the Holy Spirit. We use these words to tell what the Holy Spirit wants to say to those who put their trust in Him. But the person who is not a Christian does not understand these words from the Holy Spirit. He thinks they are foolish. He cannot understand them because he does not have the Holy Spirit to help him understand." (John 16:13-15; Ephesians 1:17)

7. *THERE ARE SOME SPECIAL THINGS THE HOLY SPIRIT DID WHILE CHRIST WAS ON EARTH.*

A. He had an important part in bringing Christ to earth and in making Christ able to do His work here on earth. John 3:34b says, "God gives Him all of His Spirit." (Matthew 1:18b; Luke 1:35)

B. He was there when Jesus was baptized in the Jordan River, and He came down from heaven like a dove. (Luke 3:22; John 1:32)

C. He was with Christ when He was tested by the devil in the desert. (Luke 4:1-13)

D. He was there when God showed that He had put His hand on Christ and had chosen Him. (Isaiah 61:1; Luke 4:16-21)

E. He was the One Who taught men when Christ spoke to them. (John 3:3-6; 14:25-26)

F. His power was able to heal people. (Acts 10:38)

G. He showed His power in Christ's life. (Luke 4:14-15)

H. He had a part in raising Christ from the dead. Romans 8:11 says, "The Holy Spirit raised Jesus from the dead. If the same Holy Spirit lives in you, He will give life to your bodies in the same way."

I. He told men they were guilty of their sins. The followers of Jesus knew they were guilty of sins and they trusted Christ. The Holy Spirit must have told them this.

The most important thing to remember is that the Holy Spirit, as one part of the Three-in-one God, has always been and always will be. The Holy Spirit was doing things before Christ came in the flesh to this earth. The Holy Spirit did things during the time Christ was on earth. The Holy Spirit is doing things today, and the Holy Spirit will do things forever.

THE WORK OF THE HOLY SPIRIT IN PEOPLE

1. THE WORK OF THE HOLY SPIRIT IN SINNERS

A. He does not live in the sinner. (John 14:17)

B. He works with people to make them want to put their trust in Christ. (John 16:6-11) He will not always do this. John 6:44 says, "The Father sent Me. No man can come to Me unless the Father gives him the desire to come to Me. Then I will raise him to life on the last day."

C. He shows the world about sin. John 16:9 says, "He will show the world about sin, because they do not put their trust in Me."

D. He tells sinners not to turn away from God, but asks them to come to God. Hebrews 3:7-10 says, "The Holy Spirit says, 'If you hear His voice today, do not let your hearts become hard as your early fathers did when they turned against Me. It was at that time in the desert when they put Me to the test. Your early fathers tempted Me and tried Me. They saw the work I did for forty years. For this reason, I was angry with the people of this day. And I said to them, "They always think wrong thoughts. They have never understood what I have tried to do for them." ' "

E. He makes God's Word alive. John 6:63 says, "It is the Spirit that gives life. The flesh is of no help. The words I speak to you are spirit and life."

F. He tells sinners the truth that Jesus is the One Who saves from sin. Acts 5:30-32 says, "The God of our early fathers raised up Jesus, the One you killed and nailed to a cross. God raised this Man to His own right side as a leader and as the One Who saves. He makes it possible for the Jews to be sorry for their sins. Then they can turn from them and be forgiven. We have seen these things and are telling about them. The Holy Spirit makes these things known also. God gives His Spirit to those who obey Him."

G. He gives power to the Word of God as it is preached to sinners. I Corinthians 2:4, 13 says, "What I had to say when I preached was not in big sounding words of man's wisdom. But it was given in the power of the Holy Spirit." "We speak about these things also. We do not use words of man's wisdom. We use words given to us by the Holy Spirit. We use these words to tell what the Holy Spirit wants to say to those who put their trust in Him." (I Thessalonians 1:5)

H. He is the *Spirit of Life* making men free from the power of sin and death. Romans 8:2 says, "The power of the Holy Spirit has made me free from the power of sin and death. This power is mine because I belong to Christ Jesus."

I. He takes away sin and gives new life. Titus 3:5 says, "...by saving us from the punishment of sin. It was not because we worked to be right with God. It was because of His loving-kindness that He washed our sins away. At the same time He gave us new life when the Holy Spirit came into our lives."

2. *THE WORK OF THE HOLY SPIRIT IN CHRISTIANS*

A. The Holy Spirit gives new life. II Corinthians 5:17 says, "For if a man belongs to Christ, he is a new person. The old life is gone. New life has begun." (John 3:5-6; I Corinthians 6:11; Titus 3:5)

B. The Holy Spirit sets the believer free from sin and death. Romans 8:2 says, "The power of the Holy Spirit has made me free from the power of sin and death. This power is mine because I belong to Christ Jesus."

C. The Holy Spirit makes the Christian's heart strong. Ephesians 3:16 says, "I pray that because of the riches of His shining greatness, He will make you strong with power in your hearts through the Holy Spirit."

D. The Holy Spirit leads Christians to a life set apart for God. Romans 8:14 says, "All those who are led by the Holy Spirit are sons of God."

E. The Holy Spirit tells Christians that they are children of God. Romans 8:16 says, "For the Holy Spirit speaks to us and tells our spirit that we are children of God."

F. The Holy Spirit brings fruit in the life of the Christian. Galatians 5:22-23 says, "But the fruit that comes from having the Holy Spirit in our lives is: love, joy, peace, not giving up, being kind, being good, having faith, being gentle, and being the boss over our own desires. The Jewish Law is not against these things."

G. The Holy Spirit leads the Christian into all truth. John 16:13 says, "The Holy Spirit is coming. He will lead you into all truth.

He will not speak His own words. He will speak what He hears. He will tell you of things to come." (I John 2:20)

H. The Holy Spirit helps the Christians to remember things Christ said. John 14:26 says, "The Helper is the Holy Spirit. The Father will send Him in My place. He will teach you everything and help you remember everything I have told you."

I. The Holy Spirit shows Christians things about God and helps them understand. I Corinthians 2:9-14 says, "The Holy Writings say, 'No eye has ever seen or no ear has ever heard or no mind has ever thought of the wonderful things God has made ready for those who love Him.' God has shown these things to us through His Holy Spirit. It is the Holy Spirit Who looks into all things, even the secrets of God, and shows them to us. Who can know the things about a man, except a man's own spirit that is in Him? It is the same with God. Who can understand Him except the Holy Spirit? We have not received the spirit of the world. God has given us His Holy Spirit that we may know about the things given to us by Him. We speak about these things also. We do not use words of man's wisdom. We use words given to us by the Holy Spirit. We use these words to tell what the Holy Spirit wants to say to those who put their trust in Him. But the person who is not a Christian does not understand these words from the Holy Spirit. He thinks they are foolish. He cannot understand them because he does not have the Holy Spirit to help him understand." (Isaiah 64:4; 65:17)

J. The Holy Spirit makes the Christian able to tell to others the Good News in power. Acts 6:10 says, "Stephen spoke with wisdom and power given by the Holy Spirit. They were not able to say anything against what he said." I Corinthians 2:1-5 says, "Christian brothers, when I came to you, I did not preach the secrets of God with big sounding words or make it sound as if I were so wise. I made up my mind that while I was with you I would speak of nothing except Jesus Christ and of His death on the cross. When I was with you, I was weak. I was afraid and I shook. What I had to say when I preached was not in big sounding words of man's wisdom. But it was given in the power of the Holy Spirit. In this way, you do not have faith in Christ because of the wisdom of men. You have faith in Christ because of the power of God."

K. The Holy Spirit helps, leads, and gives power to the Christian in prayer. Jude 20 says, "Dear friends, you must become strong in your most holy faith. Let the Holy Spirit lead you as you pray." (Romans 8:26-27; Ephesians 6:18)

L. The Holy Spirit leads the Christian to honor and give thanks to God. Ephesians 5:18-20 says, "Do not get drunk with wine. That leads to wild living. Instead, be filled with the Holy Spirit. Tell of your joy to each other by singing the Songs of David and church songs. Sing in your heart to the Lord. Always give thanks for all things to God the Father in the name of our Lord Jesus Christ."

M. The Holy Spirit helps the Christian to worship God in a good and true way. Philippians 3:3 says, "The act of becoming a Jew has nothing to do with us becoming Christians. We worship God through His Spirit and are proud of Jesus Christ. We have no faith in what we ourselves can do."

N. The Holy Spirit calls Christians and tells them to go and do special kinds of work. Acts 13:2,4 says, "While they were worshiping the Lord and eating no food so they could pray better, the Holy Spirit said, 'Let Barnabas and Saul be given to Me for the work I have called them to.' " "They were sent by the Holy Spirit to the city of Seluecia. From there they went by ship to the island of Cyprus."

O. The Holy Spirit leads the Christian even in the small things of life each day. (Where to go, what to do and what to say.) Acts 8:29 says, "The Holy Spirit said to Philip, 'Go over to that wagon and get on it.' " (Acts 16:6-7)

P. The Holy Spirit gives life to the body of the Christian. Romans 8:10-11 says, "If Christ is in you, your spirit lives because you are right with God, and yet your body is dead because of sin. The Holy Spirit raised Jesus from the dead. If the same Holy Spirit lives in you, He will give life to your bodies in the same way."

Q. The Holy Spirit gives gifts to Christians to help them work better for Him. (I Corinthians 12)

THE WORK OF THE HOLY SPIRIT IN THE CHURCH

The church is made up of all people who have put their trust in Christ. The Holy Spirit was given to the church fifty days after Jesus went up to heaven from the earth. Acts 2:1-4 says, "The followers of Jesus were all together in one place fifty days after the special religious gathering to remember how the Jews left Egypt. All at once there was a sound from heaven like a powerful wind. It filled the house where they were sitting. Then they saw tongues which were divided that looked like fire. These came down on each one of them. They were all filled with the Holy Spirit. Then they began to speak in other languages which the Holy Spirit made them able to speak."

The living church of Christ cannot be seen since it is not a building. It may be thought of as a body. Jesus Christ is the Head, and Christians are all parts of the body. Since Christ is the Head, He tells the body what to do. He does this by the Holy Spirit Who lives in the lives of Christians. The church, or all Christians, is the home of the Holy Spirit. He lives and moves in the church.

1. WHAT THE HOLY SPIRIT DOES THROUGH THE CHURCH.

A. The Holy Spirit started the church as we know it today. (Acts 2:1-4) He gave it power, and it is to show the power of the Holy Spirit to the whole world. The church is Christ's body and He is the Head. Ephesians 1:22-23 says, "God has put all things under Christ's power and has made Him to be the head leader over all things of the church. The church is the body of Christ. It is filled by Him Who fills all things everywhere with Himself."

B. The Holy Spirit lives in the lives of Christians and Christians make up the church. (Ephesians 2:19-22) What is true of each Christian must be true of all the church. I Corinthians 6:19-20 says, "Do you not know that your body is a house of God where the Holy Spirit lives? God gave you His Holy Spirit. Now you belong to God. You do not belong to yourselves. God bought you with a great price. So honor God with your body. You belong to Him." (II Corinthians 6:16)

C. The Holy Spirit rules over the church and leads it. (Acts 15:28)

D. The Holy Spirit is making the church complete by calling people to God. These are the people who put their trust in Christ to save them from sin. The church is to preach the Good News about

Christ to all people. The Holy Spirit then works in the hearts of the people they preach to. He calls them, but they must decide to follow or not to follow. Mark 16:15-16 says, "He said to them, 'You are to go to all the world and preach the Good News to every person. He who puts his trust in Me and is baptized will be saved from the punishment of sin. But he who does not put his trust in Me is guilty and will be punished forever.' "

2. *WHAT THE HOLY SPIRIT GIVES THE CHURCH TO HELP IN ITS WORK*

A. The *gifts* of the Spirit help in the work of the church. They give power. Ephesians 4:11-12 says, "Christ gave gifts to men. He gave to some the gift to be missionaries, some to be preachers, others to be preachers who go from town to town. He gave others the gift to be church leaders and teachers. These gifts help His people work well for Him. And then the church which is the body of Christ will be made strong." (Romans 12:6-8; I Corinthians 12:4-11)

B. The *fruit* of the Spirit shows the kind of work done for God. The fruit of the Spirit is love. Joy is love singing. Peace is love resting. Not giving up is love working. Being kind is showing love to others. Being good is allowing God's love to work. Having faith is love trusting. Being gentle is love with no pride. Being the boss over our own desires is love in action. (Galatians 5:22-23)

The gifts of the Spirit and the fruit of the Spirit are not the same, but work together.

PART 5

WHAT THE WORD OF GOD TEACHES ABOUT ANGELS AND DEMONS

[*Angelology*]

CHAPTER PAGE

GOOD ANGELS

Angels are beings who do not have bodies. They receive their power from God but are not all-powerful as He is.

1. *WHERE ANGELS COME FROM.*

   Angels were made (brought into being) by a powerful work of God. In Colossians 1:16 it says, "Christ made everything in the heavens and on the earth. He made everything that is seen and things that are not seen. He made all the powers of heaven. Everything was made by Him and for Him." They were made before men, but it is not known when they were made. Nehemiah 9:6 says, "You alone are the Lord. You made the heavens, the heaven of heavens with all their angels. You have made the earth and all that is on it, and the seas and all that is in them. You give life to all of them, and the angels of heaven bow down to You."

2. *ANGELS HAVE AN IMPORTANT PLACE.*

   Angels are different from men and are better in all ways than men are (in this life). In Hebrews 2:7a it says, "You made him so he took a place that was not as important as the angels for a little while." Angels are not all-powerful, do not know all things, and are not everywhere at one time.

3. *ANGELS ARE NOT LIKE PEOPLE.*

   A. They listen to God and do what He says. Psalm 103:20 says, "Praise the Lord, you powerful angels of His who do what He says, obeying His voice as He speaks!"

   B. Angels are able to tell men what will happen and what they should do. Acts 27:23-24 says, "I belong to God and I work for Him. Last night an Angel of God stood by me and said, 'Do not be afraid, Paul. You must stand in front of Caesar. God has given you the lives of all the men on this ship.' " (Genesis 19:15-22; Matthew 2:13-14; Luke 2:9-14)

   C. Angels desire to look into the secrets of how men can be saved from sin. I Peter 1:12b says, "The Holy Spirit Who was sent from heaven gave them power and they told of things that even the angels would like to know about."

D. Angels are God's helpers. In Hebrews 1:14 it says, "Are not all the angels spirits who work for God? They are sent out to help those who are to be saved from the punishment of sin."

E. When angels were brought into being, they had no sin. Some of the angels chose to fight against God and were thrown out of heaven along with Satan. But the angels who chose to stay holy as God made them are called *holy* angels. Jude 6 says, "Angels who did not stay in their place of power, but left the place where they were given to stay, are chained in a dark place. They will be there until the day they stand before God to be told they are guilty."

F. Angels are spirits but are able to do their work by using a body when they need to. Many times they can be seen by men and even look like men. John 20:12 says, "She saw two angels dressed in white clothes. They were sitting where the body of Jesus had lain. One angel was where His head had lain and one angel was where His feet had lain." (Genesis 19:1-11; 32:1-2; Matthew 1:20; Luke 1:26)

G. Angels are not held back by locked doors. In Acts 12:7-9 it says, "All at once an angel of the Lord was seen standing beside him. A light shone in the building. The angel hit Peter on the side and said, 'Get up!' Then the chains fell off his hands. The angel said, 'Put on your belt and shoes!' He did. The angel said to Peter, 'Put on your coat and follow me.' Peter followed him out. He was not sure what was happening as the angel helped him. He thought it was a dream."

H. Angels do not marry. Mark 12:35 says, "When people are raised from the dead, they do not marry and are not given in marriage. They are like angels in heaven."

I. Angels do not die. In Luke 20:36a it says, "They cannot die anymore. They are as the angels and are sons of God.

J. Angels are strong.

(1) They have greater power and strength than men. II Peter 2:11 says, "Angels are greater in strength and power than they. But angels do not speak against these powers before the Lord." (II Kings 19:35)

(2) John saw an angel having great power. Revelation 18:1 says, "Then I saw another angel coming down from heaven. He had much power. The earth was made bright with his shining greatness."

(3) An angel rolled the stone back from Christ's grave. Matthew 28:2-3 says, "At once the earth shook and an angel of the Lord came down from heaven. He came and pushed back the stone from the door and sat on it. His face was bright like lightning. His clothes were as white as snow."

THE WORK OF GOOD ANGELS

1. *ANGELS HAVE AN IMPORTANT WORK IN DOING WHAT GOD WANTS DONE FOR THE CHRISTIAN AND THE SINNER.*

A. The Law of God was given through angels. Acts 7:53 says, "You had the Law given to you by angels. Yet you have not kept it." (Galatians 3:19; Hebrews 2:2)

B. Angels lead things being done in the nations. "At that time the great angel Michael, who watches over your people, will rise up. And there will be a time of trouble, the worst since there was a nation. But at that time, every one whose name is written in the Book will be taken out of the trouble" (Daniel 12:1).

C. Angels watch over people.

(1) An angel helped Elijah. I Kings 19:5 says, "When he lay down and slept under the juniper tree, an angel touched him. The angel said to him, 'Get up and eat.' "

(2) An angel shut the lions' mouths. Daniel 6:22a says, "My God sent His angel and shut the lions' mouths. They have not hurt me... ."

(3) An angel led Peter out of prison. Acts 12:7-9 says, "All at once an angel of the Lord was seen standing beside him. A light shone in the building. The angel hit Peter on the side and said, 'Get up!' Then the chains fell off his hands. The angel said, 'Put on your belt and shoes!' He did. The angel said to Peter, 'Put on your coat and follow me.' Peter followed him out. He was not sure what was happening as the angel helped him. He thought it was a dream."

(4) Angels have the job of watching over Christians. Psalm 34:7 says, "The angel of the Lord stays close around those who fear Him, and He takes them out of trouble." Psalm 91:11 says, "For He will have His angels care for you and keep you in all your ways." (II Kings 6:15-17)

D. Angels take God's children to heaven. Luke 16:22 says, "He was taken by the angels into the arms of Abraham."

E. When Christ returns, angels will be with Him. Matthew 25:31 says, "When the Son of Man comes in His shining greatness, He will sit down on His place of greatness. All the angels will be with Him." II Thessalonians 1:7 says, "He will help you and us who are suffering. This will happen when the Lord Jesus comes down from heaven with His powerful angels in a bright fire."

F. Angels will do what God wants done to sinful people who have not been saved from sin. Matthew 13:47-50 says, "The holy nation of heaven is like a big net which was let down into the sea. It gathered fish of every kind. When it was full, they took it to the shore. They sat down and put the good fish into pails. They threw the bad fish away. It will be like this in the end of the world. Angels will come and take the sinful people from among those who are right with God. They will put the sinful people into a stove of fire where there will be loud crying and grinding of teeth." (Matthew 13:39-42)

G. Angels hold back God's anger on men. Revelation 7:1-3 says, "After this I saw four angels. They were standing at the four corners of the earth. They were holding back the four winds of the earth so no wind would blow on the earth or the sea or on any tree. I saw another angel coming from the east. He was carrying the mark of the living God. He called with a loud voice to the four angels who had been given power to hurt the earth and sea. The angel from the east said, 'Do not hurt the earth or the sea or the trees until we have put the mark of God on the foreheads of the servants He owns.' "

H. Angels will gather God's people together. Matthew 24:31 says, "He will send His angels with the loud sound of a horn. They will gather God's people together from the four winds. They will come from one end of the heavens to the other."

I. Angels will not allow men to worship them but will have men worship God. Revelation 19:10 says, "Then I got down at his feet to worship him. But he said to me, 'No! Do not worship me. I am a workman together with you and your Christian brothers who tell of their trust in Christ. Worship God.' " (Revelation 22:8-9)

2. *ANGELS CAN BE EVERYWHERE.*

A. The place where angels are most of the time is in heaven, but they can do their work on earth. Mark 12:25b says, "...They are like angels *in heaven.*" Matthew 28:2a says, "At once the earth shook and an angel of the Lord *came down from heaven.*" Luke 1:11 says, "Zacharias saw an angel of the Lord *standing on the right side of the altar* where the special perfume was burning." (Numbers 22:22-31)

B. In Jacob's dream, he saw angels *coming and going from heaven.* (Genesis 28:12)

3. *THERE ARE MORE ANGELS THAN MAN IS ABLE TO UNDERSTAND.*

A. Jesus could have called more than 70,000 angels before He was to be put on the cross. Matthew 26:53 says, "Do you not think that I can pray to My Father? At once He would send Me more than 70,000 angels."

4. *THE BIBLE SPEAKS OF TWO ANGELS HAVING NAMES.*

A. Michael - This name means *who is like God.* He is called a head angel in Jude 9. In Revelation 12:7 it says that he will fight against Satan. (Daniel 10:12-14)

B. Gabriel - This name means *the one who always wins for God.* Luke 1:19, 26a says, "The angel said to him, 'My name is Gabriel. I stand near God. He sent me to talk to you and bring to you this good news.' " "Six months after Elizabeth knew she was to become a mother, Gabriel was sent from God to Nazareth." (Daniel 8:16-26; 9:21-22)

5. *THREE SPECIAL GROUPS OF ANGEL-LIKE BEINGS.*

A. Cherubim - special bodies of honor. (Genesis 3:24; Hebrews 9:5)

B. Seraphim - these are only mentioned once and that is in Isaiah 6:2.

C. Living beings - spoken of in Revelation 4 and 5. (Ezekiel 1:5-9)

DEMONS AND THEIR LEADER

1. DEMONS ARE SATAN'S HELPERS.

A. Demons are spirits without bodies. They are bad angels who work for Satan. (Matthew 12:26-27; 25:41; Mark 1:23; 32-34; Revelation 16:13-16)

B. Demons have the power to mix up men's minds. They can make men's bodies sick. (Matthew 12:22; 17:15-18; Luke 13:16)

C. Demons know that Jesus Christ is the Son of God. They even call Him "The Holy One of God," but they do not worship Him. There is no hope for them. One day they will be thrown *into the fire that lasts forever.* (Mathew 25:41; 8:28-32; Mark 1:22-24; Acts 19:15; James 2:19)

D. Demons have an important part in Satan's place of rule. Ephesians 6:12 says, "Our fight is not with people. It is against the leaders and the powers and the spirits of darkness in this world. It is against the demon world that works in the heavens."

E. Demons spread false teaching and fight against God's plan and His people. (Ephesians 6:12; I Timothy 4:1-3; I John 4:1-6) The Word of God tells in many places about demons and how men worship them. I Corinthians 10:20 says, "I am saying that the people who do not know God bring gifts of animals in worship. But they have given them to demons, not to God. You do not want to have any share with demons." Demons help in the work of witchdoctors, and witchcraft is done in all parts of the world today. (Deuteronomy 32:17; I Samuel 28:7-20; Psalm 106:36-37)

2. THERE ARE TWO DIFFERENT GROUPS OF DEMONS.

A. The demons who are now traveling the heavens and the earth. (Ephesians 6-12)

B. The demons who are now tied up but will be loose to hurt men in the last days during *The time of much trouble.* (Revelation 9:1-21; 16:13-16)

3. SATAN IS THEIR LEADER.

Satan, who is also known as *the Devil,* is the leader of the demons.

He is the great enemy of God and man. (Matthew 12:26-27; 25:41) There are so many demons that no one can count them. (Mark 5:9)

4. *WHAT SATAN IS LIKE.*

He is a killer. He does not tell the truth because he is the father of lies. Satan has the power of death, and he is the leader of the world now. (John 8:44; 14:30; Hebrews 2:14; I John 3:8) Satan hates both God and man. (Job 1:6-12; Zechariah 3:1; Matthew 13:19, 39; John 13:2; Acts 5:3; II Corinthians 11:3; Ephesians 6:11-12; I Peter 5:8)

5. *SATAN'S NAMES:*

A. devil (Revelation 12:9; 20:2)

B. snake (Revelation 12:3, 7; 13:2; 20:2)

C. Lucifer - the morning star - the one who carries light. (Isaiah 14:12)

D. man of sin (II Thessalonians 2:8)

E. the tempter (Matthew 4:3; I Thessalonians 3:5)

F. the god of this world (II Corinthians 4:4)

G. the leader of the powers of darkness (Ephesians 2:2)

H. the leader of this world (John 12:31; 14:30; 16:11)

I. liar and murderer (John 8:44)

J. Apollyon (Revelation 9:11)

K. Abaddon (Revelation 9:11)

THE WORK OF SATAN AND DEMONS

Looking into the way demons work is not a study that brings happiness. But for the Christian who is obeying the Word of God and living daily to please the Lord, there need be no fear. Demons can work on Christians, but most of their work is done in those who have never put their trust in Christ.

1. *WHAT DEMONS ARE ABLE TO DO.*

A. Demons are able to have power over the body of a man. Luke 4:35 says, "Jesus spoke sharp words to the demon and said, 'Do not talk! Come out of him!' When the demon had thrown the man down, he came out without hurting the man." (Luke 8:29; Acts 19:16)

B. Demons are able to leave and return to the body of a man. Matthew 12:43-45 says, "When a demon is gone out of a man, it goes through dry places to find rest. It finds none. Then it says, 'I will go back into my house from which I came.' When it goes back, it sees that it is empty. But it sees that the house has been cleaned and looks good. Then it goes out and comes back bringing with it seven demons more sinful than itself. They go in and live there. In the end that man is worse than at first. It will be like this with the sinful people of this day."

C. Demons are able to bring sickness to the body. Luke 13:16 says, "Should not this Jewish woman be made free from this trouble on the Day of Rest? She has been chained by Satan for eighteen years."

D. Demons are able to bring sickness to the mind. Mark 5:5 says, "Night and day he was among the graves and in the mountains. He would cry out and cut himself with stones."

2. *HOW DEMONS START THEIR WORK.*

A. Drugs are full of danger. These and strong drink make a person so that his mind is an easy place for demons to work. (I Corinthians 10:20-21)

B. Demons can take over a mind that has turned against God. (Matthew 12:43-45)

C. Through fear. (II Timothy 1:7; Romans 8:15)

D. Hating someone without wanting to forgive them is a way that lets demons work in a person. II Corinthians 2:10-11 says, "If you forgive a man, I forgive him also. If I have forgiven anything, I have done it because of you. Christ sees me as I forgive. We forgive so that Satan will not win. We know how he works!" Luke 11:4 says, "Forgive us our sins, as we forgive those who sin against us. Do not let us be tempted." (Matthew 5:43-48; 6:14-15; Mark 11:25-26; Luke 6:36-37; Hebrews 12:15; James 3:14-15)

WHAT THE CHRISTIAN IS TO DO ABOUT DEMONS

Christians should remember that they are at war at all times with the devil. They need always to be ready to stand up against Satan.

The Bible tells what should be done to keep demons from being able to work. In James 4:7 it says, "So give yourself to God. Stand against the devil and he will run away from you." Christians are to watch out for him. I Thessalonians 5:22 says, "Keep away from everything that even looks like sin." There is no place in the Bible that gives the idea that the Christian can stand against the devil. Christians have no Biblical grounds to talk with Satan or his demons, but turn him over to the power of the Holy Spirit in the name of Jesus Christ. (I Peter 5:8-11; Jude 9)

The Christian need not worry about demons using their power on him to take over his mind. They can - and do - work on a Christian, but their power is held back because the Christian belongs to God. The Christian can at any time call upon the blood of Christ to cover him from the power and actions of demons. (Revelation 12:11)

Ephesians 6:10-17 says, "This is the last thing I want to say: Be strong with the Lord's strength. Put on the things God gives you to fight with. Then you will not fall into the traps of the devil. Our fight is not with people. It is against the leaders and the powers and the spirits of darkness of this world. It is against the demon world that works in the heavens. Because of this, put on all the things God gives you to fight with. Then you will be able to stand in that sinful day. When it is all over, you will still be standing. So stand up and do not be moved. Wear a belt of truth around your body. Wear a piece of iron over your chest which is being right with God. Wear shoes on your feet which are the Good News of peace. Most important of all, you need a covering of faith in front of you. This is to put out the fire-arrows of the devil. The covering for your head is that you have been saved from the punishment of sin. Take the sword of the Spirit which is the Word of God."

POWERFUL WORKS (FALSE) DONE BY THE HELP OF SATAN

There have always been those who have done what looked to be powerful works (miracles), but it was done by the power of Satan and is called *magic.* Such things are spoken of in the Word of God as sinful. Deuteronomy 18:9-14 says, "When you go into the land the Lord your God gives you, do not learn to follow the hated and sinful ways of those nations. There must not be found among you anyone who makes his son or daughter pass through the fire, or uses secret ways, or does witchcraft, or tells the meaning of special things, or is a witch, or uses secret power on people, or helps people talk to spirits, or talks to spirits himself, or talks with the dead. For the Lord hates whoever does these things. And because of these hated things, the Lord your God will drive them out from in front of you. You must be without blame before the Lord your God. For these nations that you are about to take listen to those who do witchcraft and use secret ways. But the Lord your God has not allowed you to do so." (II Corinthians 6:17)

1. *MAGIC IS DONE IN THESE WAYS:*

A. Telling what will happen in the future. (Genesis 44:5; Hosea 4:12)

B. Telling what will happen in the future by talking with the spirits of dead people. (I Samuel 28:8; I Chronicles 10:13-14; II Chronicles 33:6)

C. Telling what will happen in the future from certain things that happen. (Ezekiel 21:21)

D. Fooling people (magic). (Genesis 41:8; Exodus 7:11; Daniel 4:7)

E. Deciding what to do by drawing numbers.

F. Black art (magic with a desire to hurt people)

PART 6

WHAT THE WORD OF GOD TEACHES ABOUT MAN

[*Anthropology*]

CHAPTER PAGE

WHERE MAN CAME FROM

One question that has been asked through the years is, "Where did man come from?" Man has always wanted to know who made the first man and how he was made. There is no secret Who made him and what he was made from because the Bible tells all about it.

1. *STORIES OF MAN*

The Word of God is very plain in teaching that *man was made* by God, and that he was made a man *all at once by a powerful work of God.* God's Word says this, but still, people in different nations of the world have made up false stories about where man came from. Some sinful men who did not believe God's Word made up the story that man came from animals through a lot of changes. Birds, fish, and animals all have some things that are much alike. The way they breathe, their blood, their hearts, their stomachs, are alike in some ways. When some people, who do not believe God, look at these things, they say that one living thing grew to become a different living thing. Then that living thing grew to become a different living thing. This kept going on, these people say, until man came into being. These people do not teach that God made man, but that man became man through lots of changes that happened to animals over a long time. This is called *evolution* and should never be read or studied as truth.

Man is different from the animals. Man has been man since God made him from the dust. Would it not be just as easy for God to make a man as to make an animal? God's Word says that all living animals on the earth would give birth to animals of the same kind. (Genesis 1:24-25) Man cannot become one of these animals. None of the animals can become man. No one has ever proven that man came from any animal. People who do not believe in God or do not believe that His Word is true have made up false stories to try to take the power and greatness away from God.

2. *WHAT GOD SAYS*

In Genesis 2:7 it tells how man was made, and in Genesis 2:21-22 it tells how woman was made. The Word of God teaches that when the first man and woman were brought into being, they were the first of their kind and were made from nothing like them. The words used in the Hebrew language do not mean *to grow from* or *to be changed from.* Those who believe that man came from an animal like to teach that man *grew* from an animal or man *changed* from an animal. This is not what God's Word teaches! In Genesis 2:7 it teaches that the body of the first man was made from dust. Then God breathed into man the breath of life and man became a living soul. The Word of God tells that the first man and woman, Adam and Eve, were made by God at one time by a powerful work and were the beginning of the human family.

3. *OTHER THINGS THAT SHOW GOD MADE MAN:*

A. Words and writings have been handed down from the first people of nations and family groups which tell how man came from one place at one time in Central Asia. All people of the earth have the same kind of blood. In Acts 17:26 it says, "He made from one blood all nations who live on the earth. He set the times and places where they should live."

B. All the more important languages came from the same place.

C. All men everywhere in the world are much the same in the things they do and how they act.

D. People from different nations are able to have children with each other. The body of a person from one part of the world is just as warm as a person from another part of the world. The heart beat is the same with all people of the world. All people can get the same diseases. These things are not true with different animals. It is easy to see in the Word of God how the first man was made and when he was made. In Genesis 1:27 it says, "And God made man in His own likeness. In the likenss of God He made him." Man is different from animals because he was made like God.

WHAT MAN IS LIKE

1. *MAN IS MADE OF THREE PARTS - BODY, SOUL, AND SPIRIT.*

The Word of God teaches that man is made of three parts, one part is seen, and the other two parts are not seen. In I Thessalonians 5:23b it says, "May your *spirit* and your *soul* and your *body* be kept complete." This picture may help in understanding how each man has three parts.

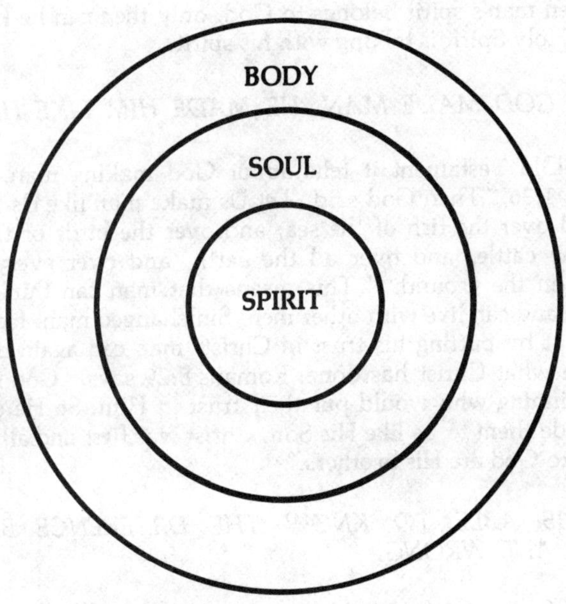

The body is made up of flesh, bones, fat and blood. The soul and the spirit cannot be seen. There is a soul and there is a spirit. Luke 1:46-47 speaks of the difference between soul and spirit. Hebrews 4:12 says, "It cuts straight into where the soul and spirit meet and it divides them."

A. The *body* of man is that which can be seen. God has made the body so that it has life. It can see, hear, smell, taste, and touch things.

B. The *soul* part of man is that which is often called the heart of man. It is not the heart of a man because the heart is flesh. The soul of man cannot be seen. In Luke 6:45 it says, "Good comes from a good man because of the riches he has in his heart. The mouth speaks of what the heart is full of." All of man's actions come from his heart. The soul does three things: it knows, it feels, and it chooses.

C. The *spirit* of the man is a part which cannot be seen. It is a very important part because it is by man's spirit that he can know God. In Romans 8:16 it says, "For the Holy Spirit speaks to us and tells our spirit that we are children of God." To begin with, man's spirit is at war with God. It needs to be at peace with God. But this can only happen when he puts his trust in Jesus Christ. When man's spirit belongs to God, only then can he know when the Holy Spirit is talking with his spirit.

2. *WHEN GOD MADE MAN, HE MADE HIM LIKE HIMSELF.*

In the Old Testament it tells about God making man. It says in Genesis 1:26, "Then God said, 'Let Us make man like Us and let him be head over the fish of the sea, and over the birds of the air, and over the cattle, and over all the earth, and over everything that moves on the ground.' " This means that man can think and have feelings and can live with other men. Sin changed man. He is not like God. But by putting his trust in Christ, man can again be like God through what Christ has done. Romans 8:29 says, "God knew from the beginning who would put their trust in Him. So He chose them and made them to be like His Son. Christ was first and all those who belong to God are His brothers."

3. *MAN IS ABLE TO KNOW THE DIFFERENCE BETWEEN RIGHT AND WRONG.*

A. The first man (Adam) knew the difference between right and wrong. The first man, Adam, knew God. Yet Adam chose to do wrong and not obey God. (Genesis 3:6-7)

B. Man today knows the difference betweeen right and wrong. Romans 2:15b says, "Their own hearts tell them if they are guilty." (Acts 24:16; I Corinthians 10:25, 27, 28; I Timothy 1:19; Hebrews 10:22; I Peter 3:16) Titus 1:15 says, "All things are pure to the man with a pure heart. But to sinful people nothing is pure. Both their minds and their hearts are bad." God's Word tells them they are wrong. (II Timothy 4:3) Man's heart is able to tell him what is right or wrong as the Holy Spirit speaks to him.

C. Man is able to choose. Every person has the power to choose. Ephesians 2:3a says, "At one time all of us lived to please our old selves. We gave in to what our bodies and minds wanted." (I Peter 4:3) Man can choose Christ as His Lord and the One Who saves from sin by putting his trust in Him, or he can turn away from Him. John 1:12-13 says, "He gave the right and the power to become children of God to those who received Him. He gave this to those who put their trust in His name. These children of God were not born of blood and of flesh and of man's desires, but they were born of God."

GOD TESTED MAN

God tested man long ago and He still tests men today. A test is a question or a problem given so that the one who is giving the test can find out something about the one being tested. After God made man, He gave him a choice. If Adam chose right, he would receive pay from God. If Adam chose wrong, he would be punished. God told Adam and Eve in Genesis 2:8-17 not to eat of one tree in the Garden. He did not give them a reason. God does not have to give men reasons for what He says to do or not to do. God just said, "Do not eat of that tree." Adam chose the wrong way. (Genesis 3:6-7)

1. *WHY DID GOD TEST MAN?*

A. God made man to be able to choose right from wrong and He wanted him to be able to choose not to sin. God made man to *honor* Him. God wants man today to love Him and serve Him because they want to.

B. God wanted to test man to see if he would obey or disobey Him. Since God made man, He had the right to test him.

C. It is sure that whatever God did, He did it for man's own good. If Adam had chosen not to sin, he could have had many great things from God. Since he did choose to sin, he led all men away from God. Men disobey God today just as Adam did long ago.

2. *WHAT DID MAN DO WITH THIS TEST?*

God let Satan tempt Adam and Eve to sin so that God could know if man would obey Him. Adam and Eve sinned (they followed Satan) and so God knew that Adam and Eve did not pass the test. God knew that all people are like Adam and Eve. All people have sin in them and do not pass God's test unless they put their trust in Jesus Christ Who is the One Who saves. Man needs God. Man needs God's loving-favor. Even when man sins, God still shows His loving-favor. Romans 5:20b and 21a say, "But where sin spread, God's loving-favor spread all the more. Sin had power that ended in death. Now, God's loving-favor has power to make men right with Himself."

MAN SINNED AGAINST GOD

1. *SATAN IS THE ONE WHO TEMPTED MAN.*

When man was made, Satan had already been put out of heaven. Satan's work was to make man sin against God. Satan had a way of fooling Eve by turning the truth of God into a lie. He made himself into a snake and came and talked to Eve. Satan tried to trap Eve and tempt her to sin. When she did sin, she tempted her husband Adam into sinning also. Since Adam was the head of all other people who would live after him, Satan was working hard to make him sin. (Genesis 1:26-28) Adam was the one God trusted to lead all other people. (Genesis 2:16) But his sin made sinners of all people. God's Word makes it clear that all people are sinners because of Adam's sin. Romans 5:12-14 says, "This is what happened: Sin came into the world by one man, Adam. Sin brought death with it. Death spread to all men because all have sinned. Sin was in the world before the Jewish Law was given. But sin is not held against a person when there is no Law. And yet death had power over men from the time of Adam until the time of Moses. Even the power of death was over those who had not sinned in the same way Adam sinned. Adam was like the One Who was to come." (Romans 5:15-19)

2. *HOW SATAN TEMPTED EVE.*

A. He made sin look good to the *body*. Eve saw that the tree was good for food. (Genesis 3:6a)

B. He made sin look good to the *mind*. She saw that the tree looked good to the eyes. (Genesis 3:6b) Eve's mind was tempted because she thought the fruit of the tree would make her wise. (Genesis 3:6c)

C. He made sin look good to the *spirit*. Adam and Eve shared with God through their spirits. Satan tempted Eve in her spirit by telling her that the fruit of the tree would make them *as gods knowing good from bad.* (Genesis 3:5) In this way, all of Eve, her body, soul, and spirit, was tempted.

3. *SIN BROUGHT A CHANGE TO EVERYTHING THAT HAD BEEN PERFECT.*

Because of the sin of Adam, many things changed:

A. Man could not share with God in the same way anymore. Before Adam's first sin, God and Adam walked and talked together. But after the first sin, Adam and Eve hid from God. They knew that God was no longer pleased with them because they did not obey God. Adam and Eve felt shame because of their sin. Their own hearts told them they were guilty. (Genesis 3:8-11; 22-24)

B. Men were no longer without sin or guilt. When God first made man, he was holy and without sin and guilt. Death came into the world because of Adam's sin. (Romans 5:12)

C. Men's bodies began to die. God had told men this would happen after they sinned. (Genesis 3:19) I Corinthians 15:22 teaches that sickness and the death of the body is part of the punishment for sin. (Genesis 2:17; 3:19; Job 2:6-7; Romans 6:23; II Timothy 1:10)

D. Even the ground changed because of Adam's sin. God allowed weeds to grow and men today cannot keep them from taking over the ground. When Jesus Christ comes back again to rule, the ground will be returned to the way it was when God first made the earth. (Genesis 3:17-19; Romans 8:20-22)

E. Because of their first sin, Adam and Eve were put out of the Garden of Eden, and man had to begin working for a living. (Genesis 3:23-24)

4. *SIN CAME TO ALL MEN.*

A. All men, everywhere, are sinners before God. Romans 3:9-11 says, "What about it then? Are we Jews better than the people who are not Jews? Not at all! I have already said that Jews and the people who are not Jews are all sinners. The Holy Writings say, 'There is not one person who is right with God. No, not even one! There is not one who understands. There is not one who tries to find God.' " (Psalm 14:2; Romans 5:12; 3:19b; Galatians 3:10; Ephesians 2:3)

B. Men are under the power of sin and Satan. Ephesians 2:3 says, "At one time all of us lived to please our old selves. We gave in to what our bodies and minds wanted. We were sinful from birth like all other people and would suffer from the anger of God." (Romans 7; John 8:31-36)

5. *SIN BROUGHT DEATH.*

In Genesis 2:17b it says, "For the day you eat from it you will die for sure." Adam did eat of the fruit of that tree and sin came into all the world and death came to all people. In Romans 5:12 it says, "This is want happened: Sin came into the world by one man, Adam. Sin brought death with it. Death spread to all men because all have sinned." There are three kinds of death. The Bible talks about all three and it is important to understand the difference.

A. Death of the body is when the heart and breath stops. The body no longer has life. In II Peter 1:14 it says, "I know that I will soon be leaving this body." (II Corinthians 5:1-5)

B. Death which divides the spirit from God came about because of Adam's sin. He was no longer able to share and talk with God. Because all people are children from Adam, all are born with their spirit divided from God and stay that way until they are saved. (Romans 5:12-19) Man can have new life through Jesus Christ and again share and talk with God. Then his spirit is no longer divided from God.

C. Death that lasts forever means being kept from God forever. It does not destroy the person, but he is kept away from God and he knows it. This death is for those who have never put their trust in Jesus Christ. (Revelation 20:6, 14, 15) Those who do not have their names written in the book of life will be put into the lake of fire forever. Those who have their names written in the book of life will have life that lasts forever. Luke 16:19-31 teaches that men die, with their soul and spirit divided from their bodies. Lazarus had been dead. His spirit was no longer in his body. But he had put his trust in Christ before he died and his spirit was with God. The rich man had not put his trust in Christ before he died, so his spirit was kept away from God forever.

PART 7

WHAT THE WORD OF GOD TEACHES ABOUT SIN

[*Hamartialogy*]

CHAPTER PAGE

WHAT SIN IS

1. *WHAT GOD'S WORD SAYS ABOUT SIN.*

Sin is:

A. Doing anything that is not right. This means the desire to sin, and the acts of sin that men do. I John 5:17a says, "Every kind of wrong-doing is sin."

B. Not obeying God's Law. I John 3:4a says, "The person who keeps on sinning is guilty of not obeying the Law of God."

C. Not doing what should be done. James 4:17 says, "If you know what is right to do but you do not do it, you sin."

D. Not believing or trusting in Christ. John 16:8-9 says, "When the Helper comes, He will show the world the truth about sin. He will show the world about being right with God. And He will show the world what it is to be guilty. He will show the world about sin, because they do not put their trust in Me."

2. *THE HOLY WRITINGS TELL WHAT SIN IS BY THE WORDS USED FOR SIN.*

In the Old Testament three words are used for sin.

A. Sin - This word means *to miss the mark.* It also means *anything short of what God expects or wants done* or *falling short of what should be full or complete.* It is not only the acts of sin but the sinful thoughts and plans of the mind. (Genesis 4:7; Exodus 9:27; Psalm 51:2, 4; Proverbs 8:36)

B. Transgression - This word means *to turn against someone and not obey the one who is boss.* (Deuteronomy 9:12; Psalm 51:2-3)

C. Iniquity - This word means *not straight.* It is not so much the act of sin as it is the way people are sinful in their hearts. (Genesis 6:5; Psalm 32:5)

In the New Testament four words are used for sin.

A. Sin - This word means the same thing in the New Testament that it means in the Old Testament. It is used 174 times in the New Testament. It means both the act of sin and the way people are sinful in their hearts. (Romans 3:23)

B. Transgression - This means *not doing what has been told to be done,* or *not obeying God and His Laws.* (I Timothy 2:14)

C. Fault - This means *to fall instead of stand,* or *not being able to do what is known to be right and should be done.* (Galatians 6:1; James 4:17)

D. Error - This means *not to know what should have been learned and known.* (Hebrews 9:7)

3. *WHAT SIN IS LIKE*

Sin is like cancer. The sinful old self causes a person to do sinful acts. Every time a person pleases his sinful old self, more acts of sin come out in his life. When cancer starts in a person, if it is not taken care of, it spreads and takes over in his body. Cancer brings death. In the same way, if sin is not taken care of, it will spread. Then the person will have death that lasts forever. (Romans 6:23; James 1:14-15)

4. *THERE IS A DIFFERENCE BETWEEN THE POWER OF SIN AND SINS.*

Most of the time sins are thought of as stealing, lying, becoming angry and many things like that, and that is what these are for sure. But the power of SIN is what makes the person want to do such things. Sin is the *want to,* or *the desire for what is wrong.* A PERSON IS NOT A SINNER BECAUSE HE SINS. HE SINS BECAUSE HE IS A SINNER. It is easy to sin because man was born with a desire to sin. It is a power that works in him, and he can do nothing to get it out of him by himself.

When a man steals something from another man he is doing something wrong against the other man. It is sin. But the reason he stole was because of the power of SIN in his life. He did not only do something wrong against the other man, he sinned against God by doing what God said should not be done.

A man may think it is sin only if it is found out. But it was sin when he first thought about it.

When a person is saved, he must be saved from the power of SIN. The power that makes him want to do wrong must not be allowed to work in him.

A person may feel the need to be saved because of some sin he has done. He may feel sorry, and pray to be forgiven, but he may be doing this only because of that one sin. He must understand that he should ask to have the power of SIN taken out of his life. If this is not done, he will find himself doing the same sin again as well as other sins. He must understand that he has to be saved from the heart of the SIN problem.

WHERE SIN CAME FROM AND WHERE IT IS

1. *WHERE SIN CAME FROM*

A. The Bible says that sin came into the world by the devil who was the head leader of bad angels. (Isaiah 14:12-17; Revelation 12:7-9) This head leader of angels, called Lucifer, was a special angel. He lived in heaven with other angels who worked for God. Lucifer was a very beautiful angel. He became proud, and said he would be like the Most High God. He wanted to sit where God sits. Lucifer sinned by wanting his way and not God's way. Five times in Isaiah 14:13-14 Lucifer says, "I will." The fifth time in Isaiah 14:14b Lucifer says, "I will make myself like the Most High." The Bible does not say how this sin came to be in Lucifer. All it says is that Lucifer wanted to be like God. God had to punish Lucifer for this sin by putting him out of heaven. Ezekiel 28:15-17 says, "You were without blame in your ways from the day you were made until sin was found in you. Through all your trading you were filled with bad ways, and you sinned. So I have sent you away in shame from the mountain of God and I have destroyed you and driven you out from the stones of fire, O cherub who kept watch. Your heart was proud because of your beauty. You made your wisdom sinful because of your beauty. So I threw you to the ground. I laid you in front of kings for them to see you." God also said that the devil would be punished in hell.

Revelation 12:9 says that Lucifer, the old snake, tried to fight God, but he lost. He and his bad angels were thrown down to earth. He was then called the *devil* or *Satan.* Jesus said that the devil is the father of lies. It was the devil who brought sin into the world. (Genesis 3:1-7; John 8:44; I John 3:8)

2. *WHERE SIN IS*

A. In the heavens: Because of the fall of Satan and his angels, sin was in heaven and it was necessary that heaven be made pure. Christ did this with His blood. (Hebrews 9:23-24) The heavens (the sky) is where Satan and his demons work now. They make war with the Christian. Ephesians 6:11-12 says, "Put on the things God gives you to fight with. Then you will not fall into the traps of the devil. Our fight is not with people. It is against the leaders and powers and the spirits of darkness in this world. It is against the demon world that works in the heavens." But there is a day coming when he will be put out of the heavens and will be on the earth. (Revelation 12:7-12)

B. On the earth: Because of the sin of Adam and Eve, sin is on the earth.

(1) Plants suffer. (Genesis 3:17-18) Weeds grew then, and men have not been able to do away with them. (Revelation 22:3)

(2) Animals and men suffer. Since the flood men and animals have been afraid of each other. (Genesis 9:2) But during the time when Christ will return to rule the earth, they will be at peace with each other. (Isaiah 11:6-9) The day the new heavens and the new earth will appear all suffering will be gone forever. Things will be perfect again. (Romans 8:19-23; Revelation 21:1-5)

C. In man: Before Adam sinned, he was able to share together in a perfect way with God. After he sinned, he had nothing to share:

(1) With God. He lost the right to share with God. (John 3:3; I Corinthians 2:14; Ephesians 4:18)

(2) With God's Law. His soul became sin-sick. (Genesis 6:5-12; 8:21; Psalm 94:11; Jeremiah 17:9; Romans 1:19-31; 7:18; 8:7-8)

(3) With man. Sin changed man's feeling toward other people. (Genesis 4; Titus 3:3)

D. Sin is in all of man - spirit, soul, and body.

(1) Man's spirit has been divided from God because of sin. In Ephesians 4:18 it says, "Their minds are in darkness. They are strangers to the life of God. This is because they have closed their minds to Him and have turned their hearts away from Him." Sin brought man down to a place where his desires are to please himself. In I Corinthians 2:14 it says, "But the person who is not a Christian does not understand these words from the Holy Spirit. He thinks they are foolish. He cannot understand them because he does not have the Holy Spirit to help him understand." Man must be born again in order to know the things of God.

(2) Man's soul has been hurt by sin. Man's own heart is not truthful to himself. (Jeremiah 17:9) The thoughts of man's heart are sinful. (Genesis 6:5, 12; 8:21; Psalm 94:11; Romans

1:19-31) Man's sinful mind works against God. (Romans 8:7-8) Man's desire is to sin. (Romans 7:18)

(3) Man's body became weak and will die because of sin. Romans 8:13a says, "If you do what your sinful old selves want you to do, you will die in sin."

3. *THINGS THAT SHOW SIN*

A. God's Word tells the truth about sin.

Romans 3:23 tells that *all have sinned.*

Galatians 3:22 says *all men are guilty of sin.*

John 1:29 tells about *the sin of the world.*

(I Kings 8:46; Psalm 143:2; Proverbs 20:9; Ecclesiastes 7:20)

B. God's Word gives a word picture of the sin of the whole man.

Head - Isaiah 1:5, "...Your whole head is sick."

Eyes - II Peter 2:14, "Their eyes are full of sex sins."

Mouth - Romans 3:14, "Their mouths speak bad things against God. They say bad things about other people."

Lips - Romans 3:13, "Whatever they say is like the poison of snakes."

Tongue - Romans 3:13, "They tell lies with their tongues." James 3:6, "The tongue is a fire. It is full of wrong. It poisons the whole body."

Neck - Jeremiah 19:15b, "...because they have made their necks hard and would not listen to My Words."

Ears - Acts 7:51a, "You have hard hearts and ears that will not listen to me!"

Hands - Isaiah 1:15, "Your hands are full of blood."

Feet - Proverbs 1:16, "Their feet run to sin and hurry to kill."

From head to foot - Isaiah 1:6 "From the bottom of the foot even to the head, there is no good part."

Bones - Habakkuk 3:16, "My bones began to waste away."

Mind - Romans 1:28, "Their minds were sinful and they wanted only to do things they should not do."

Thoughts - Genesis 6:5, "Then the Lord saw that man was very sinful on the earth. Every plan and thought of the heart of man was sinful always."

C. The earth tells the truth about sin. Romans 8:22 says, "We know that everything on earth cries out with pain the same as a woman giving birth to a child."

D. God's Law tells the truth about sin. The Law shows men how sinful they are. (Romans 3:20) Even Paul thought he was free from sin until he looked into the mirror of God's Law. (Romans 7:7-8)

E. What men see in their own lives shows the truth about sin.

Moses, David, Peter, and John each saw in their own lives the truth of sin. I John 1:8 says, "If we say that we have no sin, we lie to ourselves and the truth is not in us." The truth of sin can be seen in laws made by men. Because of sin, we must have laws. False ways of worship show the truth of sin because men know there is a need for something to be done about their sin.

F. Men tell the truth about sin.

(1) Men of God tell it. Isaiah 6:5 says, "...It is bad for me, for I am destroyed! Because I am a man whose lips are unclean. And I live among a people whose lips are unclean. For my eyes have seen the King, the Lord of All." Paul said, "Christ Jesus came into the world to save sinners from their sin and I am the worst sinner" (I Timothy 1:15).

(2) Sinners tell it. Pharoah said, "I have sinned this time" (Exodus 9:27b). Achan's answer was, "It is true. I have sinned against the Lord, the God of Israel" (Joshua 7:20b). Balaam said, "...I have sinned " (Numbers 22:34a). Even Judas, who turned against Jesus, said, "...I have sinned..." (Matthew 27:4a)

All men know they are sinners, but men do not like to say so. Some try to get away from the guilt of sin by saying it is not there. Others try hard to forget it. Others try to make it sound as if it is not so bad by giving it different names. They may call it *mistakes* or *wrongs* or names like these. But that does not change the truth about sin.

THINGS THAT HAPPENED BECAUSE OF SIN

1. WHAT HAPPENED BECAUSE OF SIN.

A. When Adam and Eve sinned some changes took place. Before they sinned they did not wear clothes and they were not ashamed. But after they sinned they saw they were without clothes and became ashamed. (Genesis 3:7-10)

B. Before they sinned they had shared together with God and did not know what fear was. But after their sin they were afraid and hid themselves from God and were not able to share together with Him. (Genesis 3:10)

C. Before they sinned they lived in a beautiful garden where it was easy to grow fruits and vegetables. Adam had power over all the animals and they obeyed him. After they sinned Adam and Eve were not allowed to live in the beautiful garden. (Genesis 3:23-24) Many weeds, thorns, and thistles grew. Adam had to work very hard for their food, and he lost his power to rule over the animals. (Genesis 3:17-19)

D. Because of her part in their sin, Eve also suffered. In Genesis 3:16 it says that she would have sorrow and pain when she gave birth to children. It also says that her husband would rule over her.

E. The snake (the devil) that tricked Eve was also punished. In Genesis 3:14-15 it says that the snake would be below all other animals and would have to move around on its stomach.

F. Because of this first sin, all men through the years have suffered. Man's body, soul, and spirit changed from the way God made him. The *spirit* that once knew God is now in darkness. (Ephesians 4:18) Men are strangers to God. The *soul* does not want to do what is right. (Ephesians 4:19) The *body*, which was made perfect, can now get diseases, suffer pain, and will die. (Psalm 14:2-3; Romans 5:12; 8:6)

2. THE PUNISHMENT FOR SIN IS DEATH

A. Punishment is the pay one receives for the wrong that was done. Punishment for sin is the pain or suffering that comes to a man when he breaks God's Law. The reason for punishment is not to make a man good, but to punish a man because God says sin must be paid for. (Revelation 19:1-2)

B. Kinds of punishment - It takes only one word to tell of the punishment for sin. The Holy Writings call this death. There are three different deaths spoken of in God's Word:

(1) Death of the body - This death is the dividing of the spirit from the body. It is when the body no longer has life or breath in it. It is shown in the Holy Writings to be part of the punishment for sin. (Genesis 2:17; 3:19; Numbers 16:29; 27:3; Psalm 90:7-11; Isaiah 38:17-18; John 8:44; Romans 4:24-25; 5:12, 14, 16, 17; I Peter 4:6)

(2) Death which is the dividing of the spirit from God - The penalty placed upon man in the Garden of Eden is first of all a dividing of the spirit from God. (Ephesians 2:1-5) By this death man loses the right to be with God. (Luke 15:32; John 5:24; 8:51)

(3) Death that lasts forever - Death that lasts forever is the dividing of the soul from God forever, and the soul will receive punishment forever. (Matthew 10:28; 25:41; Hebrews 10:31; Revelation 14:11; 20:11-15)

C. Who receives the punishment for sin?

(1) The sinner will receive the pay that is promised to him in the Word of God. Romans 6:23 says, "You get what is coming to you when you sin. It is death! But God's free gift is life that lasts forever. It is given to us by our Lord Jesus Christ."

Hebrews 9:27 says that after the body dies, the sinner will come before God to be told he is guilty and he will never be able then to put his trust in Christ.

(2) Christ received the punishment for sin for those who will put their trust in Him. (Romans 5:1-2; 5:6)

PART 8

WHAT THE WORD OF GOD TEACHES ABOUT THE CHURCH

[*Ecclesiology*]

WHAT THE CHURCH IS

1. *THE CHURCH IS MADE UP OF CHRISTIANS EVERYWHERE.*

All Christians, past, present, and future, make up what is called the *church.* These are people whose sins have been forgiven and in whom the Holy Spirit lives. (Romans 1:6-7; I Corinthians 1:2; Galatians 1:13; Ephesians 5:25)

The Greek word for *church* means being called out for a group meeting. It may help to think of the church as a body. Jesus Christ is the Head, and all Christians are a part of the body. (Ephesians 5:23-24; Colossians 1:18)

2. *THE CHURCH IS A GROUP OF CHRISTIANS IN ONE PLACE.*

Many places in the New Testament it tells of a church that worships together in a certain place, such as, *the church of Jerusalem.* Paul, the missionary, started many of these churches. It is possible for people who are not Christians to be part of this group. (Galatians 1:1-2; Ephesians 1:1; Philippians 1:1; Colossians 1:2)

3. *THE WORD "CHURCH" HAS THREE OTHER MEANINGS.*

A. The word *church* can mean those who are true Christians, but are from different groups.

B. The word *church* can mean a group of people who believe and worship in the same way. These groups are known as *denominations.* These people may have many church buildings in different places where they worship. But all the people in each of these church buildings believe the same way about what the Bible says, and they desire to worship in the same way.

C. The word *church* can mean a building. When people talk about going to church they mean the building where a group of Christians worship.

4. *SOME IMPORTANT THINGS ABOUT THE CHURCH.*

A. In Ephesians 4:15-16 it says that the church is a part of Christ. He is the Head and the church is the body.

B. In Colossians 1:18 it says that Christ was raised from the dead and will never die again. We know that if the Head cannot die, the body - the church which is a part of Christ - can never die.

C. In Ephesians 3:20-21 it says that the church was brought into being to show Christ and His shining greatness to the world.

D. In Ephesians 5:23-24 it says that the church has the work of obeying and carrying out the plan of its Head, Jesus Christ.

CHURCH GOVERNMENT

1. THERE ARE THREE KINDS OF CHURCH GOVERNMENT.

A. Government by *bishops*

B. Government by *elders*

C. Government by the *Christians* themselves

The first and second ways are seen in Acts 14:23; Acts 20:17,28; Titus 1:5. But it can be seen how the third way was also used.

2. THESE THINGS CAN BE SEEN IN EACH KIND OF CHURCH GOVERNMENT.

A. Every church had the power to go to anyone of its group who had done some wrong and try to get the wrong made right. If the Christian would not turn from his sin, he would be put out of the church. The reason for this was to keep the church pure and free from sin. Matthew 18:15-17 says, "If your brother sins against you, go and tell him what he did without other people hearing it. If he listens to you, you have won your brother back again. But if he will not listen to you, take one or two other people with you. Every word may be remembered by the two or three who heard. If he will not listen to them, tell the trouble to the church. If he does not listen to the church, think of him as a person who is as bad as the one who does not know God and a person who gathers taxes." (I Corinthians 5:1-5; II Thessalonians 3:6)

B. Every church decided who should be its leaders. (Acts 1:26; 6:1-6)

CHURCH ORGANIZATION

The church is a group of Christians who have joined themselves together to worship, to learn from the Word of God, to share what they have in God with each other, and to tell the Good News to others. The Bible teaches that churches should have leaders.

1. THERE ARE TWO DIFFERENT GROUPS OF CHURCH LEADERS FOR EACH CHURCH.

A. Church leaders (elders)

(1) *What church leaders must be.* I Timothy 3:1-7 says, "It is true that if a man wants to be a church leader, he wants to do a good work. A church leader must be a good man. His life must be so no one can say anything against him. He must have only one wife and must be respected for his good living. He must be willing to take people into his home. He must be willing to learn and able to teach the Word of God. He must not get drunk or want to fight. Instead, he must be gentle. He must not have a love for money. He should be a good leader in his own home. His children must obey and respect him. If a man cannot be a good leader in his own home, how can he lead the church? A church leader must not be a new Christian. A new Christian might become proud and fall into sin which is brought on by the devil. A church leader must be respected by people who are not Christians so nothing can be said against him. In that way, he will not be trapped by the devil."

(2) *What church leaders must do.* Titus 1:5-9 says, "I left you on the island of Crete so you could do some things that needed to be done. I asked you to choose church leaders in every city. Their lives must be so that no one can talk against them. They must have only one wife. Their children must be Christians and known to be good. They must obey their parents. They must not be wild. A church leader is God's servant. His life must be so that no one can say anything against him. He should not try to please himself and not be quick to get angry over little things. He must not get drunk or want to fight. He must not always want more money for himself. He must like to take people into his home. He must love what is good. He must be able to think well and do all things in the right way. He must live a holy life and be the boss over his own desires. He must hold to the words of truth which he was taught. He must be able to teach the truth and show those who are against the truth that they are wrong."

B. Church helpers (deacons)

(1) *What a church helper must be.* I Timothy 3:8-13 says, "Church helpers must also be good men and act so people will respect them. They must speak the truth. They must not get drunk. They must not have a love for money. They must have their faith in Christ and be His followers with a heart that says they are right. They must first be tested to see if

they are ready for the work as church helpers. Then if they do well, they may be chosen as church helpers. The wives of church helpers must be careful how they act. They must not carry stories from one person to another. They must be wise and faithful in all they do. Church helpers must have only one wife. They must lead their home well and their children must obey them. Those who work well as church helpers will be respected by others and their own faith in Christ Jesus will grow."

(2) *What a church helper must do.* Acts 6:1-6 says, "In those days the group of followers was getting larger. Greek-speaking Jews in the group complained against the Jews living in the country around Jerusalem. The Greek-speaking Jews said that their women whose husbands had died were not taken care of when the food was given out each day. So the twelve missionaries called a meeting of the many followers and said, 'It is not right that we should give up preaching the Word of God to hand out food. Brothers, choose from among you seven men who are respected and who are full of the Holy Spirit and wisdom. We will have them take care of this work. Then we will use all of our time to pray and to teach the Word of God.' These words pleased all of them. They chose Stephen who was a man full of faith and full of the Holy Spirit. They also chose Philip, Prochorus, Nicanor, Timon, Parmenas and Nicholas of Antioch who had become a Jew. These men were taken to the missionaries. After praying, the missionaries laid their hands on them."

I Corinthians 12:28 says, "God has chosen different ones in the church to do His work. First, there are missionaries. Second, there are preachers or those who speak for God. And third, there are teachers. He has also chosen those who do powerful works and those who have the gifts of healing. And He has chosen those who help others who are in need and those who are able to lead others in work and those who speak in special sounds."

C. Leaders who are over many churches (bishops)

Soon after the early church was started there were leaders over several or even many churches. They were called bishops. Later other names for such leaders were presidents, presbyters, district superintendents, etc.

CHURCH MEETINGS

When Christians met together to worship God in the early church they did certain things in their meetings:

1. *THEY THANKED GOD AND TOLD HIM HOW GREAT HE WAS.*

   This was done by singing and speaking. Ephesians 5:19-20 says, "Tell of your joy to each other by singing the Songs of David and church songs. Sing in your heart to the Lord. Always give thanks for all things to God and the Father in the name of our Lord Jesus Christ."

2. *THEY PRAYED TO GOD.*

   Acts 4:23-24 says, "As soon as the missionaries were free to go, they went back to their own group. They told them everything the religious leaders had said. When they heard it, they all prayed to God, saying, 'Lord God, You made the heaven and the earth and the sea and everything that is in them.' "

3. *THEY SPOKE GOD'S WORD.*

   I Corinthians 14:3-4 says, "The man who speaks God's Word speaks to men. It helps them to learn and understand. It gives them comfort. The man who speaks in special sounds receives strength. The man who speaks God's Word gives strength to the church."

4. *THEY TALKED ABOUT GOD'S WORD.*

   Acts 13:27 says, "The people of Jerusalem and their leaders did not know Him. They did not understand the words from the early preachers. These words were read to them every Day of Rest." (Acts 15:21)

5. *THEY READ LETTERS TO THE CHURCH FROM THE MISSIONARIES, PAUL, JAMES, PETER, JOHN AND OTHERS.*

6. *THEY RECEIVED MONEY FOR OTHER CHRISTIANS WHO WERE IN NEED, AND HELPED IN SHARING THE GOOD NEWS WITH OTHERS.*

   Galatians 2:10 says, "They asked us to do only one thing. We were to remember to help poor people. I think this is important also."

Philippians 4:16-17 says, "Even while I was in the city of Thessalonica you helped me more than once. It is not that I want to receive the gift. I want you to get the pay that is coming to you later." (I Corinthians 16:1-4)

7. *THEY ATE THE LORD'S SUPPER TOGETHER.* (See Chapter 48)

8. *THEY BAPTIZED NEW CHRISTIANS.* (See Chapter 48)

Baptism in the early church took place soon after the person put his trust in Christ. It was done by one of the older Christians or church leaders. (Acts 2:38-41; 8:12, 36-38; 9:18; 10:47-48; 16:15, 33; 18:8; 19:3-5; 22:16)

A. It showed the new Christian belonged to Christ. Romans 6:3 says, "All of us were baptized to show we belong to Christ. We were baptized first of all to show His death."

B. It showed the new Christian had become a part of the body of Christ, the true church. Galatians 3:27-28 says, "All of you who have been baptized to show you belong to Christ have become like Christ. God does not see you as a Jew or as Greek. He does not see you as a person sold to work or as a person free to work. He does not see you as a man or as a woman. You are all one in Christ."

WATER BAPTISM

When a believer is baptized, he is telling the world he belongs to Christ. Water baptism does not make a person a Christian, it shows he has put his trust in Christ who died and was buried but arose from the grave. Romans 6:3-5 says, "All of us were baptized to show we belong to Christ. We were baptized first of all to show His death. We were buried in baptism as Christ was buried in death. As Christ was raised from the dead by the great power of God, so we will have new life also. If we have become one with Christ in His death, we will be one with Him in being raised from the dead to new life." Colossians 2:12 says, "When you were baptized you were buried as Christ was buried. When you were raised up in baptism you were raised as Christ was raised. You were raised to a new life by putting your trust in God. It was God Who raised Jesus from the dead." (Acts 2:41; Galatians 3:27)

The Word of God tells us we must be sorry for our sins and turn from them and put our trust in Jesus Christ before we are baptized. Acts 2:38 says, "...Be sorry for your sins and turn from them and be baptized in the name of Jesus Christ, and your sins will be forgiven..." Acts 2:41a says, "Those who believe what he said were baptized..." Acts 8:12b says, "Both men and women put their trust in Christ and were baptized."

Christ told His followers to teach and baptize all nations. Mark 16:15 says, "He (Christ) said to them, 'You are to go to all the world and preach the Good News to every person. He who puts his trust in Me and is baptized will be saved from the punishment of sin'..." Matthew 28:19 says, "Go and make followers of all the nations. Baptize them in the name of the Father and of the Son and of the Holy Spirit."

The word *baptism* means *to dip into, cover up,* or *go under.* Acts 8:38-39 says, "...Then both Philip and the man from Ethiopia went down into the water and Philip baptized him. When they *came up out of the water,* the Holy Spirit took Philip away..." (Matthew 3:6; Mark 1:9-10; John 3:23)

It is a picture of the believer being buried as Christ was buried, and being raised as Christ was raised. It shows the believer is putting away the old life as in death and being raised to new life with Christ. Only a person who has put his trust in Christ should be baptized.

Water baptism often takes place when a new Christian becomes a part of the church where he will worship. In many countries, a Christian is not talked against or hurt until he is baptized. Then his family and others often make it very hard for him and may even bring about his death.

THE LORD'S SUPPER

The Lord's Supper, often called *communion,* is an act of worship started by Christ before He died on the cross. It was done with His followers so they would remember what He was about to do. It showed His followers that the Old Way of Worship was finished and the New Way of Worship had begun.

Exodus 12 tells the story of how the Jews were told what to do so they could hurry from Egypt at night. At the supper that night, they had to do special things to get ready. To save their oldest son from death they had to kill a lamb and put its blood on the sides and top of the door and the death angel would pass over that house. Hebrews 11:28 says, "Because Moses had faith, he told all the Jews to put blood over their doors. Then the angel of death would pass over their houses and not kill their oldest sons." Later the Jews were told to remember how God helped them leave Egypt by a special religious gathering. It was called the *Passover,* meaning the angel of death passed over that house.

All the Jews took part in this special religious gathering to remember how the Jews left Egypt. Jesus had His followers make ready for this supper. (Matthew 26:17-30) In verse 19 it says, "The followers did as Jesus told them. They made things ready for this special supper." This was the *Last Supper.* As He went through each part of the supper, He showed how He Himself was that part bringing an end to the Old Way of Worship. Hebrews 10:10-12, 14, 18 says, "Our sins are washed away and we are made clean because Christ gave His own body as a gift to God. He did this once for all time. All Jewish religious leaders stand every day killing animals and giving gifts on the altar. They give the same gifts over and over again. These gifts cannot take away sins. But Christ gave Himself once for sins and that is good forever. After that He sat down at the right side of God." "And by one gift He has made perfect forever all those who are being set apart for God-like living." "No more gifts on the altar of worship are needed when our sins are forgiven." (Hebrews 9:14-15)

After Jesus went back to heaven, His followers called this act of worship *The Lord's Supper.*

1. THE PARTS OF THE LORD'S SUPPER

A. First the bread is eaten to help Christians remember how Christ's body was given for all. Luke 22:19 says, "Then Jesus took bread and gave thanks and broke it in pieces. He gave it to them saying, 'This is my body which is given for you. Do this to remember Me.' "

B. Then the drink from the fruit of the vine is taken. This helps Christians remember how Christ's blood was given to take away sins. Luke 22:20b says, "This is My blood of the New Way of Worship which is given for you." Some churches use wine and some use grape juice. The Bible says *the fruit of the vine.* Mark 14:25 says, "For sure, I tell you, that I will not drink of the fruit of the vine until that day when I drink it new in the holy nation of God."

2. *WHO SHOULD EAT THE LORD'S SUPPER*

A. Only persons who have been saved from sin should eat the Lord's Supper. A child should not take part in this worship unless he has been saved and understands what it means. (I Corinthians 11:24-25)

B. There is danger for anyone eating the Lord's Supper if his spirit is not right with the Lord. I Corinthians 11:29-30 says, "Anyone who eats the bread and drinks from the cup, if his spirit is not right with the Lord, will be guilty as he eats and drinks. He does not understand the meaning of the Lord's body. This is why some of you are sick and weak, and some have died." The important thing is to get everything right with God, and then worship the Lord.

Nowhere in God's Word does it say that eating the Lord's Supper takes away sins.

HOW THE CHURCH TAKES CARE OF PROBLEMS AND TROUBLES

The church can be what it should be and do what it should do only when there is no sin, and when every Christian in the church does his part. If there are problems and trouble in the church, the work will be slowed down. If there is sin in the lives of the Christians, the work of the church will not be done. It is important to speak to anyone who is living in sin, and this is to be done by the church. (I Corinthians 5:1-5)

1. *THE WAY A SINNING CHRISTIAN SHOULD BE HELPED* (Matthew 18:15-17)

   A. A Christian is to go to the one who has sinned and talk to him.

   B. If he does not listen to the one Christian, one or two more Christians should go and talk to him.

   C. If he does not listen to these Christians, he should be taken in front of all the Christians of the church and the trouble should be told to them. When Paul thought Peter had done something wrong, he spoke to him about it in front of all the Christians in the church. (Galatians 2:14)

   D. If he does not listen to what the church has to say, he should be put out of the church. But even yet there is hope and forgiveness if the person turns from his sinful ways and asks to be forgiven. (II Corinthians 2:5-8)

2. *WAYS TO TAKE CARE OF PROBLEMS THAT COME TO A CHURCH:*

   A. Trouble between two or more people in the church. (Matthew 18:15-17)

   B. The Christian who sins. (I Corinthians 5:4-5, 11; II Corinthians 2:6-11; 13:2; I Timothy 1:19-20)

   C. The person who says he is a Christian but who teaches lies about God and His Word. (Romans 16:17; Galatians 5:10-12; II Thessalonians 3:6; I Timothy 6:3-5; Titus 1:10-11, 13; 3:10; II John 1:10-11)

D. The Christian who turns against the church and all that is said to him. (II Thessalonians 3:6, 14-15)

E. The weak Christian (Romans 14:1-23; 15:1; Galatians 6:1)

F. The church leader or helper who sins. (I Timothy 5:19-20)

G. The Christian who joins himself to a sinner. (I Corinthians 7:39; II Corinthians 6:14-15)

The Word of God tells how to take care of problems and trouble in the church. An important lesson is seen in Hebrews 12:6, "The Lord punishes everyone He loves. He whips every son He receives." The church must also show great love when a Christian who has sinned is punished.

THE WORK OF THE CHURCH

The church is not just a group of people who choose to worship together, but it is expected to do a work for God. No such work can be done unless the Christians are living God-like lives.

The Bible speaks of the Christians as:

1. *THE SALT OF THE EARTH*

In Matthew 5:13 it says, "You are the salt of the earth." Salt is used in two ways:

A. To keep things from spoiling. This means that the Christians are to make peace among people. Mark 9:50 says, "Salt is good, but if salt loses its taste, how can it be made to taste like salt again? Have salt in yourselves and be at peace with each other."

B. To make food taste better. The Christians are to always bring out the best in others and be a help whenever they can.

2. *THE LIGHT OF THE WORLD*

Matthew 5:14 says, "You are the light of the world." The Christian shines by allowing Christ, the great Light, to shine through him. Matthew 5:15 says, "Men do not light a lamp and put it under a basket. They put it on a table so it gives light to all in the house." The church is to shine in the world. Philippians 2:15-16 says, "In that way, you can prove yourselves to be without blame. You are God's children and no one can talk against you, even in a sin-loving and sin-sick world. Take a strong hold on the Word of Life. Then when Christ comes again, I will be happy that I did not work with you for nothing."

There are two important jobs of the church:

1. *HELPING EVERY PERSON IN THE CHURCH TO BECOME A STRONG CHRISTIAN*

A. After a person has become a Christian, he is to be taught the Word of God so there will be growth. (II Timothy 4:2b) I Peter 5:1-4 says, "I want to speak to the church leaders among you. I am a church leader also. I saw Christ suffer and die on a cross. I will also share His shining greatness when He comes again. Be good shepherds of the flock God has put in your care. Do not care for the flock as if you were made to. Do not care for the flock for money, but do it because you want to. Do not be bosses over the people you lead. Live as you would like to have them live. When the Head Shepherd comes again, you will get the prize of shining greatness that will not come to an end." (Colossians 3:16; Hebrews 4:12; I Peter 2:2)

B. Every Christian is to be filled with the Holy Spirit. Ephesians 5:18 says, "Do not get drunk with wine. That leads to wild living. Instead, be filled with the Holy Spirit." (Galatians 5:16)

C. The gifts of the Spirit were given to help the Christian. (Romans 12:6-8; I Corinthians 12:6-11; Ephesians 2:21-22)

The Christian is not only saved by God's loving-favor, but he is to keep on learning more about Christ, the One Who saved him. He becomes a new place for the Holy Spirit to live. Ephesians 2:21 says, "Christ keeps this building together and it is growing into a holy building of the Lord."

2. *TELLING THE GOOD NEWS OF CHRIST*

Jesus told His followers to preach the Good News. Mark 16:15-16 says, "He said to them, 'You are to go to all the world and preach the Good News to every person. He who puts his trust in Me and is baptized will be saved from the punishment of sin. But he who does not put his trust in Me is guilty and will be punished forever.' "

The Christian is not told to take the world to Christ, but to take Christ to the world. When Christ is taken to the world, the Good News of Christ being able to save becomes the power of God to everyone who believes. Romans 1:16 says, "I am not ashamed of the Good News. It is the power of God. It is the way He saves men from the punishment of their sins if they put their trust in Him. It is for the Jews first and for all other people also."

In each of the first four Books of the New Testament and in Acts, Christ gives the word to go and teach all people.

Matthew 28:18-20 says, "Jesus came and said to them, 'All power has been given to Me in heaven and on earth. Go and make followers of all the nations. Baptize them in the name of the Father and of the Son and of the Holy Spirit. Teach them to do all the things I have told you. And I am with you always, even to the end of the world.' "

Mark 16:15-16 says, "He said to them, 'You are to go to all the world and preach the Good News to every person. He who puts his trust in

Me and is baptized will be saved from the punishment of sin. But he who does not put his trust in Me is guilty and will be punished forever.' "

Luke 24:46-48 says, "He said to them, 'It is written that Christ should suffer and be raised from the dead after three days. It must be preached that men must be sorry for their sins and turn from them. Then they will be forgiven. This must be preached in His name to all nations beginning in Jerusalem. You are to tell what you have seen.' "

John 20:21 says, "Then Jesus said to them again, 'May you have peace. As the Father has sent Me, I also am sending you.' "

Acts 1:8 says, "But you will receive power when the Holy Spirit comes into your life. You will tell about Me in the city of Jerusalem and over all the countries of Judea and Samaria and to the ends of the earth."

We do not learn from Acts 1:8 that we are to tell the Good News only in Jerusalem until all have heard, then go on to the next places - Judea and Samaria. Then after all three places are covered, go to the rest of the world. The whole world is to hear as soon as possible.

PART 9

WHAT THE WORD OF GOD TEACHES ABOUT THE LAST THINGS

[*Eschatology*]

CHAPTER PAGE

CHRIST'S SECOND COMING

It tells all through God's Word that Christ will come to earth again. Before Christ came to earth the first time, the early preachers told about it in many of the books of the Old Testament. In the first four books of the New Testament it tells of how Christ came to earth. It was all just as the early preachers wrote.

These same men of God wrote about how Christ will come to earth the second time. We have no reason to believe He will not come just as they told about it long ago.

1. *THE BIBLE SPEAKS OF CHRIST'S SECOND COMING.*

   It tells of His second coming eight times more often than of His first coming. It speaks of it 318 times in the New Testament.

2. *THE CHURCH LEADERS TAUGHT THAT CHRIST WOULD RETURN.*

   Acts 3:20 says, "He will send Jesus back to the world. He is the Christ Who long ago was chosen for you." II Thessalonians 1:7 says, "He will help you and us who are suffering. This will happen when the Lord Jesus comes down from heaven with His powerful angels in a bright fire." (James 5:8; II Peter 1:16; I John 2:28; Jude 14)

3. *THE ANGELS TOLD OF CHRIST'S RETURN*

   Acts 1:11 says, "They said, 'You men of the country of Galilee, why do you stand looking up into heaven? This same Jesus Who was taken from you into heaven will return in the same way you saw Him go up into heaven.' "

4. *JESUS TOLD OF HIS RETURN.*

   Matthew 24:27 says, "The Son of Man will come as fast as lightning goes across the sky from east to west." (Mark 13:26; Luke 21:27; John 14:3; 21:22)

The second coming of Christ is just what it says it is in plain language. Christ Himself is coming again as a person and will be seen by everyone. Revelation 1:7 says, "See! He is coming in the clouds. Every eye will see Him. Even the men who killed Him will see Him. All the people on the earth will cry out in sorrow because of Him. "

Some of the Old Testament early preachers wrote of Christ's first and second coming without telling of the many years in between. When a man looks at two mountains that are a long way off, he does not see the valley between them. They look to him as if they are close together.

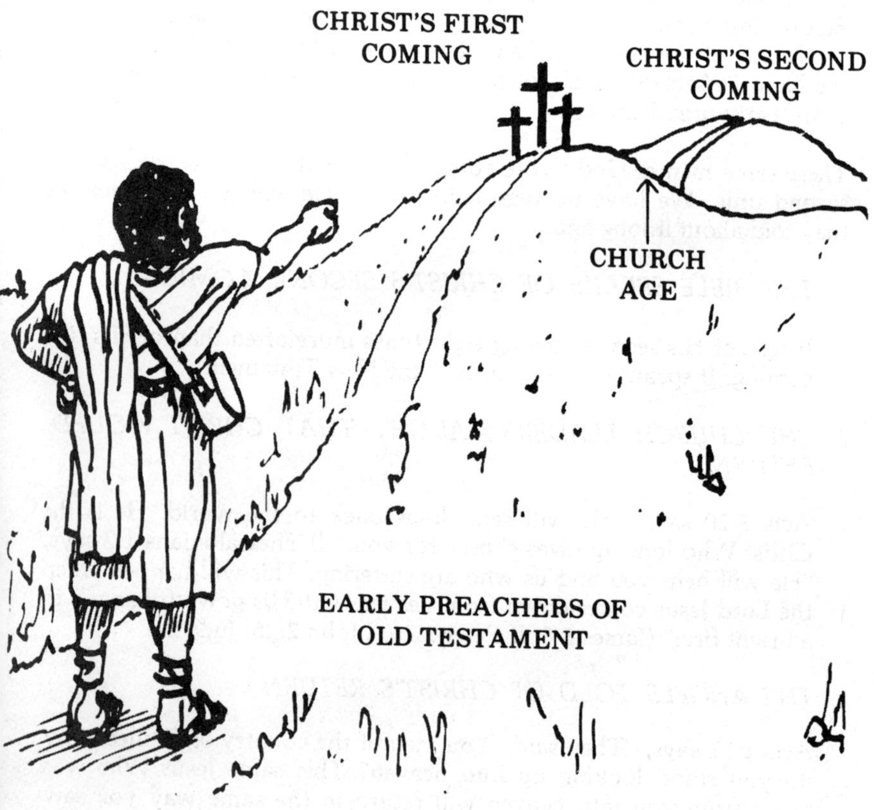

CHRIST'S SECOND COMING WILL BE AT TWO DIFFERENT TIMES

1. *FOR THE CHRISTIANS* (Rapture)

The first time Christ comes in the future, He will come *for* the Christians. During the first time He will come *in the air* (sky) and the Christians will meet him there. This is called the *rapture.* I Thessalonians 4:13-18 says, "Christian brothers, we want you to know for sure about those who have died. You have no reason to have sorrow as those who have no hope. We believe that Jesus died and then came to life again. Because we believe this, we know that

God will bring to life all those who belong to Jesus. We tell you this as it came from the Lord. Those of us who are alive when the Lord comes again will not go ahead of those who have died. For the Lord Himself will come down from heaven with a loud call. The head angel will speak with a loud voice. God's horn will give its sounds. First, those who belong to Christ will come out of their graves to meet the Lord. Then, those of us who are still living here on earth will be gathered together with them in the clouds. We will meet the Lord in the sky and be with Him forever. Because of this, comfort each other with these words."

2. *WITH THE CHRISTIANS* [*Revelation*]

The second time Christ comes in the future, He will come *with* the Christians. During this second time He will come *to the earth* where He and the church will rule the nations. This is called the *revelation.*

In Zechariah 14:4 it says, "On that day His feet will stand on the Mount of Olives, in front of Jerusalem on the east. And the Mount of Olives will be divided in two from east to west by a very large valley. Half the mountain will move toward the north and the other half toward the south."

THE TIME OF GREAT TROUBLE

1. *THERE WILL BE SEVEN YEARS OF VERY MUCH TROUBLE ON EARTH. THIS IS KNOWN AS THE GREAT TRIBULATION.*

Churches are divided as to what they believe about when Christ will return the first time.

A. The word *pre-tribulation* means that Christ will return before the seven years of much trouble.

B. The word *mid-tribulation* means that Christ will return in the middle of the seven years, or after three and one-half years of much trouble.

C. The word *post-tribulation* means that Christ will return after the seven years of much trouble.

SIGNS OF THE TIMES

Certain things show that Christ's return is in the near future. Luke 21:31 says, "In the same way, when you see these things happening, you will know the holy nation of God is near." The Word of God tells us that we should know about these things so we will not be surprised. (I Thessalonians 5:1-4) But we cannot know the day or the hour. Only God knows that. Matthew 24:36 says, "But no one knows the day or the hour. No! Not even the angels in heaven know. The Son does not know. Only the Father knows."

In Matthew 24:3-14 these signs are given:

1. *MANY PEOPLE WILL USE CHRIST'S NAME IN A FALSE WAY.* Verse 5 says, "Many people will come using My name. They will say, 'I am Christ.' They will fool many people and will turn them to the wrong way."

2. *THERE WILL BE WARS AND LOTS OF TALK ABOUT WARS.* Verses 6-7a says, "You will hear of wars and lots of talk about wars, but do not be afraid. These things must happen, but it is not the end yet. Nations will have wars with other nations. Countries will fight against countries."

3. *THERE WILL BE NO FOOD FOR PEOPLE.* Verse 7b says, "There will be no food for people."

4. *THE EARTH WILL SHAKE AND BREAK APART IN DIFFERENT PLACES.* Verse 7c says, "The earth will shake and break apart in different places."

5. *CHRISTIANS WILL BE HURT AND KILLED AND HATED.* Verse 9 says, "Then they will hand you over to be hurt. They will kill you. You will be hated by all the world because of My name."

6. *MANY PEOPLE WILL GIVE UP AND TURN AWAY.* Verse 10 says, "Many people will give up and turn away at this time. People will hand over each other. They will hate each other."

7. *MANY FALSE RELIGIOUS TEACHERS WILL START WORKING.* Verse 11 says, "Many false religious teachers will come. They will fool many people and will turn them to the wrong way."

8. *BECAUSE OF PEOPLE BREAKING THE LAWS AND SIN BEING EVERYWHERE, THE LOVE IN THE HEARTS OF MANY PEOPLE WILL BECOME COLD.* Verses 12-13 say, "Because of people breaking the laws and sin being everywhere, the love in the hearts of many people will become cold. But the one who stays true to the end will be saved."

These signs are given also:

9. *THERE WILL BE A LOT MORE SIN, BUT PEOPLE WILL SAY EVERYTHING IS FINE AND SAFE.* I Thessalonians 5:3 says, "When they say, 'Everything is fine and safe,' then all at once they will be destroyed. It will be like pain that comes on a woman when a child is born. They will not be able to get away from it."

10. *PEOPLE WILL LOVE THEMSELVES AND MONEY.* II Timothy 3:2a says, "People will love themselves and money. They will have pride and tell of all the things they have done. They will speak against God."

11. *CHILDREN AND YOUNG PEOPLE WILL NOT OBEY THEIR PARENTS.* II Timothy 3:2b says, "Children and young people will not obey their parents."

12. *PEOPLE WILL NOT BE THANKFUL AND THEY WILL NOT BE HOLY.* II Timothy 3:2c says, "People will not be thankful and they will not be holy."

13. *PEOPLE WILL NOT LOVE EACH OTHER. THEY WILL LOVE FUN INSTEAD OF LOVING GOD.* II Timothy 3:3-4 says, "They will not love each other. No one can get along with them. They will tell lies about others. They will not be able to keep from doing things they know they should not do. They will be wild and want to beat and hurt those who are good. They will not stay true to their friends. They will act without thinking. They will think too much of themselves. They will love fun instead of loving God."

14. *THE GOOD NEWS OF CHRIST WILL BE PREACHED OVER ALL THE WORLD.* Matthew 24:14 says, "This Good News about the holy nation of God must be preached over all the earth. It must be told to all nations and then the end will come."

15. *THE JEWS WILL RETURN TO THEIR HOMELAND.* Ezekiel 36:24 says, "For I will take you from the nations and gather you from all the lands, and bring you into your own land."

16. *THE JEWS WILL MAKE THE WASTE LAND BECOME LIKE A GARDEN.* Isaiah 35:1b says, "...The desert will be full of joy and become like a rose." The land of Israel is like this now, so different than it was even some years ago.

17. *PEOPLE WILL GO PLACES THEY HAVE NEVER GONE BEFORE, AND WILL KNOW MORE THAN THEY HAVE EVER KNOWN BEFORE.* Daniel 12:4b says, "...Many will travel here and there and knowledge will be more and more."

FALSE-CHRIST

Just before Christ returns to the earth with His Church, the false-christ or the person known as the *antichrist* or the *lawless one* will be given power to rule over all the earth. This time will be known as *the time of much trouble* or *the great tribulation*, and will last for seven years.

There will be much bad and wrong done in the world. This will be brought on by many false-christs. I John 2:18 says, "My children, we are near the end of the world. You have heard that the false-christ is coming. Many false-christs have already come. This is how we know the end of the world is near." Things will get worse because of the *real false-christ* taking over everything.

1. *THE FALSE-CHRIST WILL BE THE RULER OVER ALL RELIGIONS, GOVERNMENTS, AND MONEY OF THE WORLD.*

   Revelation 13:7, 15 says, "It was allowed to fight against the people who belong to God, and it had power to win over them. It had power over every family and every group of people and over people of every language and every nation." "The second wild animal was given power to give life to the false god. This false god was the one that was made to look like the first wild animal. It was given power to talk. All those who did not worship it would die."

   Satan will be his boss, and he is also called *the wild animal.* Revelation 13:2 says, "The wild animal I saw was covered with spots. It had feet like those of a bear. It had a mouth like that of a lion. The snake-like animal gave this wild animal his own power and his own throne as king. The wild animal was given much power." In II Thessalonians 2:3 he is called *the man of sin.*

2. *THE FALSE-CHRIST'S JOB WILL BE TO WORK AGAINST GOD, AND ALL THAT IS RIGHT AND GOOD.*

   He will put himself up as if he is God. He will have power over all the nations of the earth.

3. *NO ONE KNOWS WHEN THE FALSE-CHRIST WILL FIRST BE SEEN.*

   After the church is taken up to heaven and the Holy Spirit will no longer be working with people on earth, the false-christ will start his work right away. (II Thessalonians 2:6-8) But all Christians are given hope to look for *Christ, not* the false-Christ. (Luke 21:28, 36)

4. *THE FALSE-CHRIST WILL BE ALLOWED TO COME TO PUNISH THOSE WHO TURNED AWAY FROM CHRIST AND CHOSE TO TURN AWAY FROM GOD'S WORD.*

In II Thessalonians 2:11-12 it says, "For this reason God will allow them to follow false teachings so they will believe a lie. They will all be guilty as they stand before God because they wanted to do what was wrong."

THE 1,000 YEAR TIME

The word *millennium* means 1,000 years. In the first seven verses of Revelation 20, *1,000 years* is used six times.

Churches are divided in what they think the Holy Writings teach about the 1,000 year time. There are three different ideas:

1. *PREMILLENNIUM*

   Premillennium means that Christ will return before the 1,000 years. It teaches that there is a 1,000 year time to come and that Christ will return to earth before the 1,000 years. When He comes He and the Christians will rule the world. For the first 300 years the early church taught this.

2. *AMILLENNIUM*

   Amillennium means that the millennium started with the coming of Christ and goes through the whole New Testament time until the end of this age. It means that the Christians are now ruling with Christ and those who have died are ruling with Him up in heaven.

3. *POSTMILLENNIUM*

   Postmillennium means that Christ will return to earth after the 1,000 year time is over.

Two important things will take place before the 1,000 year time:

1. *THE BATTLE OF ARMAGEDDON*

   This will be a world war against God and the Jews. (Revelation 16:12-16) Christ will have power over those who make war against God because He will come down from the sky and destroy the sinful armies. (Psalm 2; Isaiah 29:1-8; Joel 3:9; Zechariah 14:1-5; 14:12-15; Revelation 19:17-21)

2. *THE NATIONS ARE TOLD IF THEY ARE GUILTY.*

   After Christ wins the war of Armageddon, He will set up His holy nation on earth and gather the nations before Him to say if they are guilty. (Matthew 25:31-46)

Some other things will happen:

1. *SATAN WILL BE TIED AND THROWN INTO THE HOLE WITHOUT A BOTTOM DURING THIS 1,000 YEAR TIME.* (Revelation 20:1-3)

2. *THE CHRISTIANS WHO HAVE BEEN RAISED FROM THE GRAVES WILL HAVE THEIR NEW SINLESS BODIES AND WILL RULE WITH CHRIST ON EARTH.* (Revelation 20:4)

3. *THE SINFUL DEAD PEOPLE WILL NOT BE RAISED FROM THE DEAD UNTIL THE 1,000 YEAR TIME IS FINISHED.* (Revelation 20:5, 12)

4. *THE JEWISH NATION WILL BECOME A LEADING WORLD POWER DURING THIS 1,000 YEAR TIME.* (Zechariah 8:23; 14:8, 9, 16; Romans 11:23-32)

The 1,000 year time and what will happen to the church, the Jews, and the nations:

1. *THE CHRISTIANS WILL RULE WITH CHRIST.*

   This would also mean that those who suffered for Christ during the time of much trouble will rule with Christ. Revelation 20:4 says, "Then I saw thrones. Those who were sitting there were given the power to say who is guilty. I saw the souls of those who had been killed because they told about Jesus and preached the Word of God. They had not worshiped the wild animal or his false god. They had not received his mark on their foreheads or hands. They lived again and were leaders along with Christ for 1,000 years."

2. *GOD MADE A PROMISE TO DAVID WHICH HAS NEVER BEEN BROKEN.*

   God promised that the throne on which David sat to rule his nation would be kept forever, and that David would never want a man to sit on it. (II Samuel 7:11-17; Jeremiah 33:17) When Christ came to earth as a baby in the town of Bethlehem, He had the right to take that throne. (Luke 1:32) When Christ will return and rule on earth, He will use that same throne. (Isaiah 9:6-7) The house of God that David built will be built again. (Acts 15:16) The Jews will be a respected and honored people on the earth. (Zechariah 8:13)

3. *THE BATTLE OF ARMAGEDDON*

   This will take place before the 1,000 year time and will not kill all the people of the earth, but only those armies that are fighting in that battle. There will be people living in other parts of the world who will say Who Christ is. Romans 14:11 says, "The Holy Writings say, 'As I live, says the Lord, every knee will bow down before Me. And every tongue will say that I am God.' " If every knee does bow down before Christ, it does not mean that all these nations will put their trust in Christ. It is one thing to bow down before Him and another to put one's trust in Him. If any nation does keep on fighting against God and will not obey, that nation will be punished right away. (Zechariah 14:16-19) The important thing for that time will be holy living. (Zechariah 14:20-21)

The reason for the 1,000 year time:

1. *THE 1,000 YEAR TIME WILL BE WHEN GOD WILL TEST MAN THE LAST TIME.*

   The 1,000 year time is not what the Christians are looking forward to. They are looking forward to the Holy City, the new Jerusalem. (Revelation 21:9-22) This 1,000 year time will be when God will test man the last time. Things will be better then because Satan will be tied and out of the way and Christ will be ruling.

2. *THE 1,000 YEAR TIME WILL BE A GREAT TIME FOR THE JEWS.*

   Micah 4:6-7 says, " 'In that day,' says the Lord, 'I will gather together those who cannot walk and those who have been driven away, even those whom I have made to suffer. I will make a new beginning with those who cannot walk. I will make a strong nation of those who have been driven away. And the Lord will rule over them in Mount Zion from that day and forever.' " There will be peace over all the earth. (Isaiah 2:2-4; Micah 4:3-4) There will be lots of money, food, and things. (Isaiah 35) All animals will get along well together. (Isaiah 11:6-9) Christ will rule all things well. What He says and does will be right. (Isaiah 11:1-4)

After the 1,000 years Satan will be let loose for awhile. He will go around lying to the nations. Many people will follow him. Soon after he will be thrown into the lake of fire. (Revelation 20:10) The earth and the heaven will leave. In Revelation 20:11 it says, "Then I saw a great white throne. I saw the One Who sat on it. The earth and the heaven left Him in a hurry and they could be found no more." This is, no doubt, what Peter wrote about in II Peter 3:7-10. Then the great white throne where God sits will be seen, and those who have never put their trust in Christ will be told they are guilty. (Revelation 20:11-15) The One Who will sit on that great white throne is Christ Jesus. (John 5:22; Acts 17:31)

PEOPLE WILL BE RAISED FROM THE DEAD AND TOLD IF THEY ARE GUILTY

1. *THE 1,000 YEAR TIME WILL NOT BE THE END OF THE WORLD.*

Before the end of the world other things will happen:

A. The Christians will be raised from their graves when Christ comes for those who have put their trust in Him. I Corinthians 15:22-23 says, "All men will die as Adam died. But all those who belong to Christ will be raised to new life. This is the way it is: Christ was raised from the dead first. Then all those who belong to Christ will be raised from the dead when He comes again." (I Thessalonians 4:14-17) This will be before the 1,000 year time. It is called the *first resurrection*. Revelation 20:6 says, "Those who are raised from the dead during the first time are happy and holy. The second death has no power over them. They will be religious leaders of God and of Christ. They will be leaders with Him for 1,000 years."

B. Those who did not put their trust in Christ will be raised from their graves after the 1,000 year time is finished. In Revelation 20:12-13 it says, "I saw all the dead people standing before God. There were great people and small people. The books were opened. Then another book was opened. It was the book of life. The dead people were told they were guilty by what they had done as it was written in the books. The sea gave up the dead people who were in it. Death and hell gave up the dead people who were in them. Each one was told he was guilty by what he had done."

2. *THE CHRISTIAN WILL STAND BEFORE GOD BEFORE THE 1,000 YEAR TIME. THIS IS KNOWN AS THE JUDGEMENT SEAT OF CHRIST.*

The Christian is not told he is guilty because God has already put that guilt on His Son, Jesus Christ, on the cross. John 5:24 says, "For sure, I tell you, anyone who hears My Word and puts his trust in Him Who sent Me has life that lasts forever. He will not be guilty. He has already passed from death into life." His sins were taken care of at the cross, and by faith in that work, he is free from the punishment of sin. But all Christians must stand before Christ. In II Corinthians 5:10 it says, "For all of us must stand before Christ when

He says who is guilty or not guilty. Each one will receive pay for what he has done. He will be paid for the good or the bad done while he lived in this body." This will take place when the church is taken up to meet the Lord in the air. The reason Christians must stand before Christ at that time is to tell what they have done in their work for Christ. (Matthew 25:14-30; Luke 19:11-27)

The *works* of every Christian will be tested by fire. Some will be burned to ashes because they are only *wood, hay, and grass.* Other *works* will stand the test, and come out as *gold, silver, and stones worth much money.* Those whose works are burned up will be saved as if they were going through a fire. I Corinthians 3:12-15 says, "Now if a man builds on the Stone with gold or silver or beautiful stones, or if he builds with wood or grass or straw, each man's work will become known. There will be a day when it will be tested by fire. The fire will show what kind of work it is. If a man builds on work that lasts, he will receive his pay. If his work is burned up, he will lose it. Yet he himself will be saved as if he were going through a fire." This will be a time when the Christian receives the pay that is coming to him for his work.

Revelation 11:18b says, "...It is time for the servants You own who are the early preachers and those who belong to You to get the pay that is coming to them. It is time for the important people and those not important who honor Your name to get the pay that is coming to them. It is time to destroy those who have made every kind of trouble on the earth." Revelation 20:8b-9 says, "He will gather them all together for war. There will be as many as the sand along the seashore. They will spread out over the earth and all around the place where God's people are and around the city that is loved. Fire will come down from God out of heaven and destroy them."

3. *THE SINNER WILL STAND BEFORE GOD AFTER THE 1,000 YEAR TIME. THIS IS KNOWN AS THE GREAT WHITE THRONE JUDGEMENT.*

The person who is not a Christian will be told he is guilty because his name is not written in *The Book of Life.* In John 14:6 Jesus said, "I am the *Way* and the *Truth* and the *Life*. No one can go to the Father except by Me." (Acts 4:12; I John 5:12)

Those who are told they are guilty will suffer punishment for sin forever. There will never be an end to the suffering. (Matthew 25:46; Mark 9:43, 48; Revelation 14:9-11)

The place of that suffering is called the *lake of fire.* (Revelation 19:20; 20:10, 15)

It should be remembered that the *lake of fire* was made ready for *the devil and his angels,* not for man. (Matthew 25:41) But those who keep on in the way of sin must suffer the same punishment as the devil and his angels.

God wants all men to be saved from the punishment of sin. He said in Revelation 22:17b, "Let the one who wants to drink of the water of life, drink it. It is a free gift." And in II Peter 3:9b He says, "...The Lord does not want any person to be punished forever." II Corinthians 6:2b says, "Now is the right time! See! Now is the day to be saved." (Isaiah 49:8)

THE NEW HEAVEN AND THE NEW EARTH

After the heavens and earth are destroyed with fire (II Peter 3:10) there will be new heavens and a new earth. (II Peter 3:13) This will be called the *Holy City* or the *New Jerusalem.*

It will be a far better place than man can think of. Only what is right and good will be there. There will be no more death, or sorrow, or crying, or pain. Everyone will be worshiping God. There will be no night there. It will be the new home for all those who have put their trust in Christ and have been saved from the punishment of their sins. (Revelation 21; 22:5)

"He Who tells these things says, 'Yes, I am coming soon!' Let it be so. Come, Lord Jesus." (Revelation 22:20)